DOOMED TO SUCCEED

Leading Nigeria into the Emerging Future

DOOMED TO SUCCEED

Leading Nigeria into the Emerging Future

AUSTIN OGUEJIOFOR AMAECHI, PhD

\ ppx executive reach publications\

NIGERIA | UK | USA | CANADA
Copyright @ 2018 by Austin Oguejiofor Amaechi

The moral right of the author has been asserted.

A CIP catalogue record for this book is available from the British Library.

ISBN (pbk)- 978-0-9930332-3-0
ISBN (ebk) - 978-0-9930332-4-7

First published in Great Britain in 2018 by PPX Executive Reach.

For further information, please contact the author through
@draustinamaechi or email info@executivereach.com

To Dr. Ifeanyi Ubah for his committed leadership in socioeconomic and human capital development, care for people with special needs and well-mannered contributions in the House of God.

And to Dr. Pastor Paul Enenche for the grace in his scholarly and life saving Seeds of Destiny Daily Devotional message. He once wrote: Until thought changes, actions and results can never change!

PREFACE

My fellow Africans, I appeal to you that though this task seems hard, it is entirely doable and we must begin this journey. Let us rise to this challenge and begin to elect leaders who we trust in and are confident will help us realize the social and economic hopes of our continent

Tony Elumelu

The nature of the workings of government depends ultimately on the men who run it. The men we elect to office and the circumstances we create that affect their work determine the nature of popular government. Let there be emphasis on those we elect to office.

Valdimer Orlando Key Jr

When you become entitled to exercise the right of voting for public officers, let it be impressed on your mind that God commands you to choose for rulers, "just men who will rule in the fear of God." The preservation of our government depends on the faithful discharge of this duty; if the citizens neglect their duty and place unprincipled men in office, the government will soon be corrupted; laws will be made, not for the public good so much as for selfish or local purposes; corrupt or incompetent men will be appointed to execute Laws; the public revenues will be squandered on unworthy men; and the rights of the citizen will be violated or disregarded. If our government fails to secure public prosperity and happiness, it must be because the citizens neglect the Divine Commands, and elect bad men to make and administer the Laws.

Noah Webster

The reason to write this book could not be more obvious. With the inauguration of Muhammadu Buhari on 29 May, 2015, Nigeria supposedly entered an era where proposition that effective and ethical leaders matter a great deal. But that has not ended the era of dishonesty among our politicians and from those given positions of power. You will be correct to say that we are living in unsettling and dangerous times. We need to learn the lessons of history.

Amidst tremendous security and strange economic challenges and preparations towards another general election cycle, there is perplexity everywhere. There is real despair in the communities about our present and past political leaders. It is time that Nigeria electorates do what good followers does. Good followers invest time and energy in making informed judgments about who their leaders are and what they espouse. Then they take the appropriate action. Our democracy of today requires continual eternal vigilance by the good and informed people of Nigeria. Paraphrasing a famous *US Senator, all of us must aspire to the courage to put the greater good above our own.* To do successfully, we must remember the words of Benjamin Burombo: *"Each time I want to fight for African rights, I use only one hand because the other hand is busy trying to keep away Africans who are fighting me."*

We, Nigerians, lack trust in the ability of our leaders to lead well and effectively. We are known to always complain about our leaders and rightly so. We eventually get rid of them, though indirectly for the most part, and move on to the next one hoping that they would be different. And it seems that they never are. We complain about the quality of the men and women who run our governments and legislate and manage the government agencies. We bemoan their incompetence, and sometimes their detachment, their lack of urgency, and their lack of empathy. We have done this to every leader or every head of government who has run the affairs of this great country.

If we consider our present and past leaders, especially at the federal level, a good question would be Why are we, Nigerians, bad at electing or picking compassionate and competent leaders? Selecting the right people to lead can be extremely difficult. It's easy to say that if we have better choices, we will pick better leaders. And let's be honest here, if we do not, it means we have been promoting the wrong people through the system.

This book has been a long time in writing. It began with a nationwide essay writing competition for undergraduate students in our Universities on the topic of: *The Essence of Excellent Leadership* first conducted in 2006. Since then, I have continuously asked questions of what we must look for in our leaders in different forums and comments accumulated over a good period of time. Summarising the rich stew of our country's men and women views on the subject has been a hazardous task. The subject is far too complex. This book is an attempt to transcreate rather than translate the participant's submissions. From the assessments of the conversations, I have isolated different leadership attributes that came up again and again.

Nigerians are victims of broken promises from our politicians and from those given positions of power. We live our lives enmeshed in complex adaptive systems; that are often described as diverse, volatile, uncertain, complex and ambiguous. No one really knows what's coming around the next corner; we're all operating on uneven footing. Many Nigerians has this view that our democracy would be near perfect if it weren't for all the people currently involved in the political leadership. This is very important because it does matter who is our president? It does matter who the state governors are. It does matter who the Senate president or house speaker are. It matters who the local government chairmen or legislators are.

It is also humorous of our society's stand that widely admired reputation equals do no wrong and capacity to govern well and presumed corruption equals corruption and no capacity to govern. It is possible that the *power causes brain damage,* phrase is real in Nigeria. Power is said to deprive leaders or those given positions of power of knowledge. What we see often from them include contempt for others, loss of contact with reality, restless or reckless actions, and displays of incompetence. Is there nothing to be done? No and yes.

There is some heartening news, however: Society's willingness to accept bad behaviour from political leadership badness seems to be dwindling.

In making that all important choice, many Nigerians are NOW suggesting that we take into consideration the candidates' different values or deep-seated beliefs that motivate behaviours; their abilities or ways of thinking and behaving or the qualities that people are endowed with, or acquire; their proficiencies; and capacity to learn or develop new capabilities. *In this context, certain character and personality traits are associated with being a good leader (integrity and wise judgment, for instance), as are particular skills and capacities (effective communication and decision making, for example).* These are values also called traits that Nigerians want to see in a candidate seeking any elective office or those given positions of power. For each, what is required is someone who can navigate adeptly through the twists and turns of turbulent times. Someone who understands that influence is maintained through cooperation, not intimidation.

An accurate understanding of reality is the essential foundation for producing good outcomes. This book seeks to facilitate a conversation. If you have a position on the gate and you don't warn the people of what you see, you're to blame. Hello Nigerians, it is very important that we stop glorifying mediocrity and ineptitude. It is very suffocating to see and read sometimes fatuous comments on our dailies and other media platforms. As Parker Palmer once said, *"we live in the present moment, with its tedium and terror, its fear and hopes, its incomprehensible losses and its transcendent joys. It is a moment in which it often feels as if nothing we do will make a difference, and yet so much depends on us."*

We must take responsibility for ourselves and take the potential consequences of our choices extremely seriously. Every action has unintended consequences. Many leaders and those given positions of power are clearly in it for themselves, but there surely are plenty who really do want the best for everyone. Critical or uncritical dissemination of labels on any individual should be avoided or treated with caution. We know that purpose-driven people act and adapt. Expertise doesn't ensure right action. Giving every one of us the ability to make informed decisions as to who should lead us is a contribution envisaged for this book. The challenge is clear. Good leadership may be the missing link in our quest for greatness, but our politicians are not lazy. Democracy is not the problem. Practising of the democracy in an era of mass ignorance is the problem.

In our society, the majority-minority looks, sounds, and thinks in vivid contrast; and not just in terms of different ethnicities, social class, religions, and sexual orientations. And most make political decisions on the basis of social identities, and not based on an alerting examination of reality. Because they're so motivated by their own goals, they expect everyone to share their passion and punish you, least by mouthing the wrong words, when you don't. But what is common is that everyone wants a future of better career opportunity and wage security than is currently the case. The challenges of modern politics are so vast and abstract that it's difficult not to find them overwhelming. Therefore, in this book, we stress that, change is needed, different from the past and present. Until thought changes, actions and results can never change. As William Faulkner once said, *"you cannot swim for new horizon until you have courage to lose sight of the shore."*

Let's get started and activists in the house would be wise not to debate nouns and verbs. Budging the uninformed from their perches takes fortitude because mentality determines reality.

Austin Oguejiofor Amaechi

THANKS AND ACKNOWLEDGMENTS

Writing a book of empowering collection of advice that advances the leadership outlook for 21 Century success, is harder than I thought and more rewarding than I could have ever imagined. Although the subject of this book has been the marketplace of leadership and followership ideas, the arguments made herein are really about changes in Nigerian politics. Like a traditional public intellectual, I am making arguments a bit afield from my principal area of expertise. None of this would have been possible without many people.

First and foremost, I would like to thank all the undergraduate university students both past and present in Nigeria universities who participated in the Excellent in Leadership easy competition. I have also been the beneficiary of an ongoing online conversation about these topics in the blogosphere and on Twitter. Even though I have not actually met many of my online interlocutors, their links, feedback, and stark benefited me tremendously during the drafting of this book. The Facebook respondents to my survey also made this project much, much easier, and I thank those very busy people for taking the time to answer my questions. Many of the ideas, notions, and actual paragraphs in the text had their origins from these sources.

This book uses numerous quoted remarks, poems and case studies. These items are not included for mere appearance and style; they significantly contribute to the effectiveness of the book in conveying certain important ideas. I would like to express my gratitude to those whose work or poems I have quoted. However, I have the sole responsibility for the interpretation placed on these poems. Where I have quoted or relied on them, I have tried to acknowledge the author in the text, but I'm sure there are some I have forgotten, and for this I apologise.

I lived through a tumultuous time when I was writing this book, to say the least. Every experience is a valuable teacher and I never take anything for granted. I had fair portion of reliable, competent, trustworthy people standing with me, however, and I thank God for that. The friendship of Dr. George Okafor has proved invaluable to me, in many ways, for many years, as has the behind-the-scenes and subtle support of precious Ogochukwu Amamchukwu, Ade Whenu, Aisha Alabakundi, and Uche Onuzulike.

Akin Makinde, Mariam Yakubu Ikunaiye and Timbo Ayinde were wonderful throughout.

Finally, I am very, very, very grateful to my family. My career decisions in the past few years have taken its toll on my children Chigozie, Chisom, Chidinma and their mother. I thank them for their support, patience and kindness.

CONTENTS

The good news is, there is light at the end of the tunnel.
The bad news is, there is no tunnel.

Shimon Peres

1

Introduction: Unto Our Own Future

It is change, continuing change, inevitable change, that is the
dominant factor in society today. No sensible decision can be made
any longer without taking into account not only the world as it is,
but the world as it will be … this, in turn, means that our
statesmen, our businessmen, our everyman must take
on a science fictional way of thinking.
Isaac Asimov

I am immensely grateful to God Who Has preserved us to witness
this day and this occasion… we face enormous challenges.
Insecurity, pervasive corruption, the hitherto unending and
seemingly impossible fuel and power shortages are the
immediate concerns. We are going to tackle them head on.
Nigerians will not regret that they have entrusted
national responsibility to us. We must not succumb to
hopelessness and defeatism. We can fix our problems.
Muhammadu Buhari

What we are doing here in Rwanda is not a miracle, nor is it
impossible elsewhere, it is simply the commitment of an entire
nation, especially Rwandan youth and women.
Paul Kagame

I charge us all to fasten our seat-belts and power on with the work we
have been tasked to do. Posterity is watching, and history will
vindicate us if we do the job with diligence and in truth.
Abubakar Bukola Saraki

EVERY AUTHOR, HAS IN MIND A SETTING in which readers of his
or her work could benefit from having read it. Mine is the same and set in

a scenario, where opinions are shared and need for personal responsibility exchanged. This book of salvos comes with a smile and simple messages: *"Questioning what we believe and want is difficult at the best of times and especially difficult when we most need to do it, but we can benefit from the informed opinions of others. And, in the end, effective actions alone are insufficient. We must look instead at what are truly meaningful actions."* And in this context, discussions on the future direction of our nation must be informed by public engagement in all regions of the country. I do not know how we are in Nigeria - given the strange and uncertain times that we are in.

Daily life in Nigeria has become enmeshed in a perpetual nightmare of violence and criminality and anxiety. How does one describe the continuous and deliberate killing of a people in a supposed safe and stable country? Each day's news cycles bring head-spinning and disturbing headlines. Some have since concluded that Nigeria democratic politics are perpetually chaotic with no vision of equality and justice and freedom. It will be impossible to move into ordered domains. Order is where the people around you act according to well-understood social norms, and remain predictable and cooperative. During the weeks before and months after the 2015 presidential inauguration, there was a definite perceptiveness that the Nigeria has come out of sustained period of crisis and is now moving forward.

All too true, alas and uh-oh. More and more so-called lazy youth and other not so lazy Nigerians are noisily questioning the country they're inheriting and demanding things work differently. There are more frustration and anger. The result is that we are dividing, and polarizing, and drifting towards chaos. Under such conditions, if we are to avoid more catastrophes, it is necessary for each of us to bring forward the truth, not the arguments that justify our ideologies, not the machinations that further our ambitions, but stack pure facts of our existence, revealed for others to see and contemplate, so that we can find common ground and proceed together.

The experiences available in Nigeria have demonstrated that effective actions are insufficient. Only meaningful action can lead to effective living. As you will discover reading this book, WE need today a different kind of leadership. The current leaders can learn and oncoming ones must come with the understanding. In my research work, I have had the privilege of talking to numerous supposedly effective people in our effective government of today. A notable observation in our discussions is some of them expressing bitterness resulting from a lack of purpose, a lack of meaning for their actions. Our leaders must distinguish between effective action and meaningful action relative to the core concern of human performance and needs of Nigerians of today and tomorrow.

Again, many of the current Nigeria political leaders are focused on the past and activists are focused on dissatisfaction. There is a lot of dissatisfaction indeed but that dissatisfaction is not really channeled in a positive and constructive way on the country's political scene. I am afraid that without constructive changes on the political level, the country cannot really progress. Mahatma Gandhi once said: *"You may never know what results come of your actions, but if you do nothing, there will be no results." What should you do, when you don't know what to do? Tell the truth is the recommendation. So, that's what we will do in the oncoming pages.*

Foreseeing New Kind of Leaders

Are you going through difficult times? If it does nothing else for you and to you, it will open the eyes of your heart. This is not a mystery book, but one that tells us about urgent need for personal responsibility and shares the thoughts of our people on what they want to see in our country's political leaders of today and tomorrow.

The ideas for this book have been in the making for the past ten years. I have posed questions of what we must look for in our leaders to our people in different forums and comments accumulated over a period of time. The first was conducted as part of a nationwide essay writing competition for the undergraduate students in Nigeria Universities on the topic of: *The Essence of Excellent Leadership first conducted in 2006.* I also synthesised discussions held on the Facebook and Twitter social media platforms. Summarizing the rich stew of comments regarding our country's men and women's views on the subject is a hazardous task. This book is an attempt to transcreate rather than translate the participant's submissions. From the assessments of the conversations, I have isolated different leadership attributes that came up again and again. These themes appear as Chapters 4 – 19 of this book, and I hope you will benefit from their contents as much as I have.

The transcreation has been a tough job. I know this isn't highly advanced research, but the results presented in this book have our people's needs, wants, and desires in mind. Nigerians are worried, grumble monotonously and rightly so.

It took a long time to settle on a title: ***Doomed to Succeed: Leading Nigeria into the Emerging Future.*** Why did that one rise up above all others? First and foremost, because of its simplicity. It indicates clearly that new leadership and citizens relationship is needed, and that chaos otherwise beckons. There is no sufficient debate on the health of our country. It is something we need to have. If we do not start this effort soon, before long we shall discover that we started too late.

A word of warning. This book is going to ask a lot of you. It has to, because leadership needs to be redefined for tomorrow. There will be times when you may feel overwhelmed by the conclusions in this book. You may feel they are completely unrealistic, but I am confident you will also realise that the transcreated opinions of fellow Nigerians as presented are ones you have already thought about.

I have dreamed of the result helping our success in electoral democracy. We have failed many times already in our choices. Although failure is a great teacher, we cannot afford the time to continue to learn from our failures. Human societies cannot be subjected to such a process. There is no harm in dreaming of that gracious effective choice or in speculating about what it might look like.

Whether in thought or action, we should dig more deeply into ourselves and think or act in a way that is somehow more highly evolved or enlightened. By definition this will not come easily. For some it will not come at all and that is another major reason for this book. Inaction tears at our conscience and will continue till a defined action is taken. The President of the European Commission, Jean-Claude Junker, noted while describing politicians that: "We all know what to do; we just don't know how to get re-elected after we've done it."

A genuine and meaningful action is focused outward. I am allergic to some sort of poetry. I expect many of my readers will be. I began every section and chapter in this book with selected poem(s). Only poets pronounced as such or not are capable of giving words commensurate with what we are experiencing both as leaders and as followers. The poet, Muhammadu Buhari is one of them. And I also regard Oby Ezekwesili, Bukola Saraki and numerous others mentioned in this book as poets. Buhari said: *"we must not succumb to hopelessness and defeatism. We can fix our problems." Saraki said: "Posterity is watching, and history will vindicate us if we do the job with diligence and in truth." Ezekwesili, said: "We must reset our political space with the entry of a new generation of people that can commit to Building a New Nigeria at every level of our society." And Ifeanyi Ubah once said: "My faith cannot be compromised by my political ambition; the Bible is littered with examples of great leaders who fell by the wayside through disobedience."* There are phrases in all of them that captured key elements of what I am talking about. I encourage you to read the poems and the book. See if it does not somehow speak to you of the kinds of meaningful actions that should stir us into a better direction. At every level, it is the duty of both leaders and followers to speak the truth and point to hope only.

Nations Rarely Kaput

Open-minded pragmatism, meritocracy, and honesty can serve as a trustworthy compass WHEN Nigerians agree that the good of the country is what really counts, but it is not in our reasoning and attitudes. Nigeria voters must face the truth. We sometimes support political leader (s), who do not have the necessary capacity to be a 21st century leader. Accepting reality is not passive - it doesn't mean giving up either.

"We must remember that the future is not only a time, but it is a place. In fact, these places of the future will be inhabited by people with innate characteristics that mirror who they were yesterday, who they are today, and who they will be tomorrow." These humorous words, attributed to *Baker* stated in her article, *The Future is about People,* help to frame the ideas discussed in this book. Additionally, Baker noted that since people will make up the future, we can assume that certain human characteristics, like the need to explore, the need for interpersonal relationships, and the need to find answers to our questions, will very likely remain. A leader's elements and characteristics such as the importance of emotional courage, meaningful communication, adapting and malleability, all of which impact leaders and followers today, are likely to have an impact into the distant future.

For many of our future challenges, our problems will lie within the hearts, minds, and behaviour of people, and so the solutions will lie there as well. Many of today's challenges are too complex to yield to the exercise of leadership alone. When we the people are the problem, the people are the solution. Take your leadership further. Inspire others for action, spark innovation. Multiply your impact. Most of our political leaders and appointees are not active. *People attend meetings and conferences, but their minds are somewhere else. Being present increases productivity, but most of our leaders are never present.* A question asked by Nigerians and expanded in chapter sixteen is: *is something neurologically wrong with our leaders?*

Have you read any of the numerous inspiring speeches given by *late Prime Minister, Abubakar Tafawa Balewa.* I urge you to seek out his speeches and learn. It is still relevant. On September 2, 1957, he is quoted to have said:

> "...Nigeria has now reached a critical stage in her history. We must seize the opportunity which has been offered to us to show that we are able to manage our own affairs properly. Every Nigerian, whatever his status, and whatever his religion, has his or her share to contribute to this crucial task. I appeal to all my countrymen and women to cooperate with me and my colleagues to create a better understanding among our peoples, to establish mutual respect, and trust, among all our tribal groups, and to unite in working together for the common cause, the cause for which no sacrifice will be too great.
>
> I am convinced, and I want you also to be convinced, that the future of this vast country must depend, in the main, on the efforts of us [ourselves] to help ourselves. This we cannot do if we do not work together in unity. Indeed, unity today is our greatest concern, and it is the duty of every one of us to work so that we may strengthen it. This morning I said in the House of Representatives that bitterness due to political differences would carry Nigeria nowhere, and I appealed to the political leaders throughout the country to control their party extremists. To you who are listening tonight I repeat that appeal - Let us put away bitterness and go forward in friendship..."

That's Abubakar Tafawa Balewa speaking in 1957, when I was not even born. That was true then and remains true today. Basic truths do not change. If and when Balewa's words are embraced by our today's leaders, the actions will deliver practical benefits. There is never a good time. My choice of timing imposes on this book many risks of error and misunderstanding. I began the transcreation work resulting to this book in a season of heartbreak – personal and career heartbreak – that soon descended into a dark night of the soul. When things go wrong, they can go wrong in a big way. But as I fumbled in the dark, the poet Roethke's words proved true time and again: *my eyes were opened to new insights, and my heart was opened to new life.*

The present is made up of people, it's equally important to remind ourselves that people will still make up the future. Nepotism (the focus of chapter six in this book) is judged to be morally wrong and Nigerians are so worried with relative ease with which it is practised in our country. That is awful. *Mr. President, Mr. Governor,* you guys must understand that Nigerians are not happy that it is happening. How can you be a great and innovative president of a country or governor of a state, when you do not know the people and their values? Please you must work harder to understand. Lakhdar Brahimi was excellent when he said: *"Understanding, I think, is the most important thing when you are dealing with people-any people. You have got to make the effort to understand even the un-understandable."*

Even though, the future is unknowable and cannot be predicted with foregone conclusion, we must still maintain our unwavering desire to prognosticate. It is time to put the people and the communities we live in first, not party politics and not personal privilege as some of our political leaders are doing today. The subject of poor leadership and governance in Nigeria continues to resist comprehension. Resist, but not defy I believe. President Buhari has the attitude to change Nigeria. But has he got the time, emotional courage, critical thinking, public support and energy? What is needed in Nigeria is not new in the world. There is a proven story available of how one man changed his nation – really created a nation - and built it with his clearly defined mission, vision and strategic leadership.

Late Prime Minister, Lee Kuan Yew, built Singapore to much of what it is today. President Buhari or whoever comes after him has a lot to learn from Lee Kuan Yew's capacity.

I have been in the field for the past three years with my research bag and I have seen that Nigerians are ready for a new kind of politics and real nation building. They are crying out for a real national leader with vision and truthfulness. President Buhari has the mantle and he is doing what can be done. More is needed. President Buhari must never allow himself or those very close to his government to split North East, North West, North Central, South West, South South and South East into "good guys" and "bad guys." It is happening and I have experienced it, and the feeling is sour and the taste really bad. Those charged with real authority ought to be worrying for all of us. They must learn to build, innovate and how best to close the widening chasm of wealth and opportunity in the country.

I have recently finished reading an inspiring *"Lincoln's Melancholy"*, written by Joshua Shenk. It is a probing examination of the sixteenth US president's journey with depression. Lincoln struggled with this affliction until the day he died. Lincoln, in his darkest time, was not thinking of his personal pains or the *good guys and bad guys* divide, but one united nation.

I appeal to our current and future presidents and governors to speak to the country more often. Lincoln was a great man and never misses an opportunity to speak to his country men and women. And by the way - this is important, swagger is not competency. Using the occasion of his second inaugural address, delivered on March 4th, 1865, a month before the end of the Civil War, Lincoln appealed for "malice toward none" and "charity for all," animated by what one writer calls an "awe-inspiring sense of love for all" which bore the brunt of the battle. In his appeal to a deeply divided America, Lincoln points to an essential fact of their life together: *"if we are to survive and thrive, we must hold its divisions and contradictions with compassion, lest we lose our democracy."* Lincoln was president during the Civil War: *North vs. South, brother against brother, black against white, neighbour against neighbour.* Role models, especially those in authority like parents and presidents, are powerful figures. Let those of us who have been chosen (or elected or by association) to lead, use that gift of power for the good of our fellow human beings, and worry less about *good guys or bad guys.*

This book, like the personal journey that helped shape the transcreated portions, does not blink at the darkness laced through Nigeria political and economic life today. Still, it is full of hope about our capacity to see the light. *As poet Theodore Roethke wrote: "In a dark time, the eye begins to see."* During my weeks and months sojourn on the dark side, it was hard to believe that my vision was growing sharper or to make sense of what I was seeing. And yet as I slowly came back to life, I found that I had gained new clarity about myself, the communities I had associated with for so many years on and that has also depended on me at their period of disengage. I feel stuck at times in the process.

Think about it. You and me, have everything we need to take the next small, realistic step forward. So embrace the opportunities that come your way, and accept the challenges.

It's All About Us

It is obvious that we have not a moment to lose, if we are looking to a 21st century Nigeria. Someone once told a story about a French general who asked his gardener to plant a tree. *"Oh, this tree grows slowly, the gardener said. It won't mature for a hundred years. Then there's no time to lose, the general answered. Plant it this afternoon."*

In our Nigeria of today, men in leadership positions are talking about change without a foreseeable end. If this inconveniences you, then name the problems, pull no punches, and agitate for egalitarian change. In the 2015 general election cycle, we saw that change only happens when ordinary people get involved and engaged, and decide together to demand for it. What the 2015 election also demonstrated is that when citizens experience economic uncertainty and its accompanying loss of personal control, they look to dominant leaders, those perceived as more agentic, forceful and decisive – over their prestige counterparts. *These, I think, are the reasons why a reasonable percentage of Nigerians as discussed in chapter nineteen of this book are demanding for enlightened autocratic leaders in our democracy.*

The experiences of the past years both at federal and various state government levels have certainly shown that there are consequences for our choices. The uninformed must be informed for our country to grow her governance outcomes. In chapter twelve, a focus is on the danger inherent in allowing people with deliberately living narcissistic into political leadership positions. Let us vote out those already elected who have obviously shown their inability and readiness to change. *George Santayana, a Spanish philosopher, said it much better: "He who doesn't understand history is doomed to repeat it."*

We have an Opportunity. Let us take it

President Buhari in his 2015 inaugural address said, "We have an opportunity. Let us take it." I want to warmly support that with a simple quote by Galileo: "eppure si riscalda (and yet it moves)." As history has it, this was Galileo's stubborn response to church inquisitors questioning his findings about the earth orbiting the sun. He is basically saying that, regardless of whether or not the inquisitors believed him, it didn't matter. It just is.

I further transcreate it to mean, even if your situation is terrible, the first step in improving it is acknowledging it for what it is. Tough times may be upon you, and if not, they are coming because that is how life goes. In the midst of tough times, you can choose to let circumstances define and defeat you or strengthen and empower you. Tough times aren't fun; they aren't even fair. However, you can choose and choose wisely. There is no misconception left that democracy is a complex, shifting and contested concept. It is happening. No inquisitor, no ideologue, no presidential decree will change that. Democracy is challenged and in some ways in decline in quality and delivery. Government and governance institutions function poorly, are falling into disrespect and are weakened by internal divisions, lack of confidence and poor leadership. We today need to be reminded that the purpose of democracy is not to be democratic but to provide for safe and meaningful government.

If you are to preside, you better be effective, if you must vote, at least make sure you know what you will get from the man or woman you are voting for and not what you assumed. In the lonely period the transcreation and book writing provided me with, I kept returning many times to the 2015 inaugural address of President Buhari and the wonderful first speech given by Abubakar Tafawa Balewa as the prime minister designate in 1957.

I keep telling others and myself that all the despair, pessimism and fear in the country are transient, and like a lonely cloud crossing a clear sky, will soon disappear.

> …as far as the constitution allows me I will try to ensure that there is responsible and accountable governance at all levels of government in the country. For I will not have kept my own trust with the Nigerian people if I allow others abuse theirs under watch…

Those were the rousing words of the President of Federal Republic of Nigeria, President Muhammadu Buhari during his inauguration. It was May 29th, 2015 and the world was watching and listening. I thought he was right saying those words. Has he kept his promises? We are all artist. Oscar Wilde was probably correct when he said: "No great artist ever sees things as they really are. If he did, he would cease to be an artist."

In years to come, President Buahri will retire from public service. When he does, someone might well say of him these words Mark Twain wrote about the 32nd US Speaker of the House, Thomas B. Reed: *"He was transparently honest and honorable, there was no furtiveness about him, and whoever came to know him trusted him and was not disappointed."*

However, President Buhari's solutions to domestic problems are where it begins and ends. President Buhari has been accused of populism over his 2015 inauguration slogan *"I belong to no one and I belong to everyone."* The president's actions and inactions in the last three years have shown him as a paradox that defied easy categorisation. The president wants to leap into the future, but he is ignoring the bombs in his path. What we are seeing at least in the past three years is a proof that changes, reforms, and transitions carry with them the seed of instability. I am not saying that everything he has done or doing is right, but I want to believe that everything he did is for an honourable purpose. There is a saying that before a leader can pull us out of despair, we have to fall into it. Nigeria is in despair.

Citizens Must Take Responsibility

The political challenges of 2018 are different from 1999. In an era of the social media, there is a greater plurality of views and ideas. Politics has become more contestable, which calls for politicians to be more adept at consultation and consensus building. The preparation of informed and concerned citizens is especially urgent due to the troubling political, educational, and sociological challenges that confront us every time we read the news and faced with family demands. Every local failure is a national failure, and we are having so many of them now. It' is no surprise therefore that raw anger, disgust, and despair contributed in the 2015 general election cycle decisions and will probably have a say on the percentage of the 2019 winning results. While some three years ago President Buhari was perceived by the public and cabal of business, political, and military leaders as a shadow coming from the past, now he looks like an ambassador coming from the future.

Are we where we should be? The answer from so many people's perspective is that we are getting there but it can be better. The old is over. I believe that government has the responsibility to allow people to fulfill their dreams. Our problems are complex and it will take a qualified leader to tackle all the issues successfully.

I believe in personal responsibility: Choices have consequences, good or bad. Every 21st century Nigerians must decide to be part of the solutions. As the future becomes less certain, scenario planning and critical thinking becomes more useful. This book is written to function in that frame of usefulness. It is written to contribute in making Nigeria democracy signal not the liberation of elites from the electorate but the liberation of the masses. The book is written to talk about what Nigerians want in Nigerian leaders and potential leaders. While we can, let us elect proper and fit persons. Rather than trying to dominate their fellow citizens, the Nigeria privileged few have simply turned their backs on them.

I believe that everybody in life has a choice. You either find solutions to the challenges you face or you keep making excuses and starve. To appropriate the words of German Chancellor Angela Merkel: "The times in which we could completely depend on others are, to a certain extent, over." It is important therefore that elected officials and voters in Nigeria are encouraged to sacrifice everything to solve the problems of appointing unsuitable officials or voting for unsuitable and unqualified leadership candidates. The performances of certain agencies of government in our country are an indicative of lack of self-awareness and Nigerians are saying something has to change. Research by *Tasha Eurich, author of best-selling book: Insight,* shows that self-awareness is the meta-skill of the 21st century. Self-aware people are more successful, more confident, build better relationships, and are more effective leaders. *Chapter eleven of this book focuses on the amazing potential of emotional courage and self-awareness.*

Great followers are great leaders and they are clear

They understand their role. You can not be a good follower unless you have clearly identified the leader. Great followers not only accept this fact, they embrace it. Fellow citizens of Federal Republic of Nigeria, it is time to reshape our country for tomorrow. We should not let the cabal of business, political, and military leaders get away with asserting they have this magic stick and magical ability when we can bore down a little deeper to see whether they have these necessary and underlying traits. That requires originality and that itself starts with creativity. Nigerians are seeking for a better nurture a culture of clarity and transparency in the governance. *Miscommunication is the main reason behind most team tensions and importance of both clarity and effective communication for a better governance are discussed in chapter seven.*

How correct are the transcreating results presented in this book. I will say; I am guided by history and toolkits. *A number of forecasting tools are available to decision makers looking to leverage the power of precise predictions. One such tool is known as Forecasting Tournaments.* In 1906, Francis Galton asked fairgoers in Plymouth, England, to predict the weight of a slaughtered ox. While individual predictions varied widely, the median of the crowd's prediction was almost exactly right. Out of this experiment came the theoretical basis for the wisdom of the crowd, which postulates that crowd-based estimates will converge on the truth because individual prediction errors are random and thus cancel when aggregated.

This book also drew interpretation on the research from the growing field of *evidence-based management and people analytics,* in which leaders and followers are encouraged to design experiments and gather data instead of relying solely on logic, experience, intuition, and conversation. Interpretation was also drawn from *crowd and social psychology fields*. The field holds that the crowd is as psychologically specific as the individual. That's not an exaggeration, that is a statistic.

Leadership today has to be about a burning desire to create a better future and to not give up in the resistance that you are going to face when you decide to do something different. We are indeed in an open-source era in which ordinary people are really empowered. Leaders, on the other hand, are totally exposed to the extent of being naked. What is important is seldom urgent, and what is urgent is seldom important. Newly elected presidents or governors do not leave their personalities on the doorstep when they enter the office. They are still basically the same people they were before being elected, but in the office of president or governor they have many more responsibilities and much more power. The impact of their decisions and actions can be enormous. That is why it is important to examine the character and competence of any present or future candidates before casting that all important vote. Character is relatively stable. Once developed, it changes slowly. If patterns of words and actions can be identified, they can help explain and to some extent even predict reactions. *Former US First Lady Michelle Obama once said:* "*...being president doesn't change who you are; it reveals who you are...*"

Thus, knowing a candidate's character provides a guide to understanding and anticipating their actions and inactions in office. Although it is a difficult subject to scientifically prove, conventional wisdom, theories of personality derived from clinical observation, psychometric measurement, social interaction, and organizational leadership on individual and group behaviour proved that our characters can and do affect the decisions we make and actions we take.

Candidates Must be Asked Tough Questions

If the citizens of Nigeria continue to neglect asking the tough questions and keep electing bad men to make and administer the nation's laws, we end up with insipid government of nothing but: selfish laws, nepotism, squandered revenues, violated rights, lost public prosperity and happiness. Nigeria leadership is every citizen's business. We should certainly be optimistic about 2019 and beyond. We have the tools we need to make things better. The question is, do we have the courage and understanding to act?

With all his flaws, Nigeria has a capable president in President Muhammadu Buhari, But ultimately and fundamentally, we must continue to explore because it is inherent in who we are. The impulse to explore, to discover and to create something new traces back to the beginning of the human race. To draw back on leadership traits exploration is to deny who we are, and who we still could become.

Any new Nigeria President either in 2023 or subsequent general elections if we are fortunate to still have the country would have his or her problems. I am thinking of the wise words of American journalist, *Lincoln Steffens, who once wrote that: "Power is what men seek, and any group that gets it will abuse it. It is the same story."*

Going Forward

Our attitude makes the difference. *We are not in any form guaranteed a better future until we acquire a better mentality.* Whether at the dinner table or in the social media, it can feel as though our opinions and mindsets are more fixed than ever. I am not being alarmist. I believe it is the facts. Look around: even the best decisions will harm some people. The first step to making these decisions: *is to understand what makes them so hard.* It is one of the reasons why this book is written to help you on. It is hard; however, I believe in the power of hard work and its capacity for leading to ultimate success.

This book is not written to tell Nigerian voters or elected or appointed officials how to do things as required by the constitution. Given our distaste for rules, this book does not provide rules. What it does is a provision of structure. It is telling us what we can achieve using our privileges. It promotes knowledge and understanding and solidarity. The book asked that we centre conversations and debates in our country on facts and facts only, and it reminds us that there are always unintended consequences on our choices.

A common theme in this book is that we live in disorienting and challenging times and we urgently need to create a new future for Nigeria. Among the current ideologues are people who pretend they know how to make the country a better place before they have taken care of their own chaos within.

The experience of the past three years has clearly shown that it's a tough time to be a political leader attempting to deploy tried and tested tools when society no longer behaves in tried and tested ways. Nigerian youth, the single largest demographic in our society today, are often derided as lazy, disrespectful, and needy. They're also criticized as being so addicted to social media. My findings in this book project do not support those conclusions.

There are many of the best of President Muhammadu Buhari in Nigeria. I and many other Nigerians are hoping that the Muhammadu Buhari that we knew yesterday and have today will find them and develop them unto our future. He whose future lies in his past has no future. If you ask me, I will say, developing the other Muhammadu Buhari starts with recruiting widely and wisely. The current recruitment patterns would not do it.

In researching this book, I found that every leadership philosophy built on one strength eventually fails eventually, because a country's economic and political transformation is, at its core, about solving problems— and there are as many ways to transformational lead as there are types of problems to solve. I can conclude as well that a nation's future is only dependent on the individuals, rather than governments. And to take a nation forward we need to focus on ourselves rather than on the political leaders.

Dear Mr. President and all others in position of power, starting and finishing well require a high degree of imagination, creative analysis, and strategic thinking competence. These are what Nigerians wants each of you to have and be.

A team will always reflect its leader and a leader no matter how manipulative you want to be is reflected in his team.

You are a current political office holder or campaigning to be elected to an office Nigerians will appreciate your view of restructuring of the country. For instance, the former vice President, Atiku Abubakar, have the view that restructuring Nigeria's economy and polity is a necessity, not an option. It will foster a spirit of freedom in a diverse nation and nurture strong and democratic government.

It All Ends. Your Destiny is Your Decision.

We have to know better today than we did yesterday in order for the present to be different from, and better than, the past. We have to keep on knowing, today, in order for the future to be different from the present. While it's crucial to care and consider your present, be careful not to let it hinder your future. You NOW get my drift in this book!

In the end, we have seen and can say that bad governance doesn't discriminate.

2

Poor Leadership | Bad Governance is Heartbreaking

Sometimes we need to start out with a blank slate and say, Hey;
we've been doing this for the last 40, 50 years. It doesn't work.
Let's throw out everything, clear out minds ... Let's have as a
goal doing the right thing for the right reasons,
even if it entails taking risks.
Vincent Lane

YOU MAY HAVE THE BEST, most important proposal, but how do you present it to someone who insists on doing things the way they've always been done? And that is the challenge we are having in Nigeria. The natural reaction when faced with a problem of any kind is to find a solution and fix it. We know we have leadership selection problem resulting to somewhat poor governance issues; and this book is written to contribute to the solution. Good governance to a large extent, is very often a choice, just like bad governance.

Leadership, by its nature, is an anxious and inconstant idea. It was US John Adams, that suggested, in a letter to a friend, that there was something both undemocratic and unwise in the lionization of leadership. The country won't improve, Adams wrote, until the people begin to "consider themselves as the fountain of power." He went on, *"They must be taught to reverence themselves, instead of adoring their servants, their generals, admirals, bishops, and statesmen."* Although don't settle for the low hanging fruit has always been regarded as a good and positive adage; if we are to participate or indeed survive in the future, our people should better get serious on our choices and decision-making.

Nigeria Is Simple Only When It Behaves

It is very difficult to make sense of the interconnected chaos of reality, just by looking at it, except if we are talking about the national football team. What we have in Nigeria is crying out for a change. Bad electoral design, bad electoral practice, not bad people, is the root problem. It is *not about inadequate or wrong-headed laws, political structure and policies, but lack of national value systems. What is the qualification for running for public office? In most countries with love of her citizens, it is most likely to be 'competence,' in Nigeria it is 'loyalty.'*

Our governing system is broken and dysfunctional and the root problem is the cause. Without public belief in our ability to rise to the daunting challenges we face, to act collectively through our democracy, the quality of self-governance goes into a vicious circle of cynicism, disaffection, and failure.

The July 24, 2018 Has Way Deeper Flaws

As have said in the introductory part of this book, the price of greatness is responsibilities. President Buhari and Vice President Prof Osibanjo couldn't have risen to be in many ways the leading team in the Nigeria without being involved in its problems, without being convulsed by its agonies and inspired by its causes. For its intent and efforts towards accountability, I still endorse the team with all its faults. What remains is working wholeheartedly for the people, and the support of the people are essential, if they are to succeed. Serving the people must not be a slogan, but a reality. It was President John Kennedy that once said: "*Our task is not to fix the blame for the past, but to fix the course for the future.*" The current president and vice president and those that will come after them, need to build up national consciousness and cultivate shared values, balance the strive for economic growth with social justice, find a way to care for vulnerable groups such as those living with neurodevelopmental disorders and strengthen the nation's soft power. The current dynamic Senate President, Sen. Bukola Saraki and the House Speaker, Rt. Hon. Yakubu Dogara and those that come after them, must do the same. That would be a good thing no matter which party controls the Senate and the

House and regardless of who is, or will be, President. How much progress can we make as a nation under the obvious politically charged environment, lack of strategic clarity and cross-functional conflict between the executive and legislative arm of the government. Not much, I think. Again, we must blame the design and practice and not the people. If the system does not change, it will not support and sustain individual behaviour change. It will even set people up to fail.

Speaking on the legacies of late Singapore Prime Minister, Lee Kuan Yau, former US Secretary of State, Henry Kissinger once said: *"The mark of a great leader is to take his society from where it is to where it has never been."* To achieve that, Nigeria must do away with ethno-centric nation building and embrace fully meritocratic vision. Ethnic politics is ugly; religious politics is dangerous. I happen to believe that these would be achieved with a greater sense of urgency and emotional courage. A good example is the best sermon.

The various political events on this particular *July 24th, 2018* in Nigeria, was not good governance in its finest. Whatever it takes to achieve good governance or the cause of lack of it, must be the ambition of each of us. There is always the possibility of contagious influence, if the events of *July, 24th, 2018* become a constant in our democracy. This book points ahead to the work to be done in every realm of our lives throughout the nation. However, everything shifts and changes in the real world.

We must accept that holding a position of authority in life is transient. Any opportunity should be seen as an opportunity to be helpful to mankind. *A certain former US Senator, Strom Thurmond, in his time, never wanted a certain particular debate to take place outside his standings. He only exited the Senate after he held a 24 hour filibuster – the longest ever at the time in hopes of stopping the Civil Rights Act of 1957. The bill easily passed two hours later.*

In complex systems, we have the assumption, that, each hypothetically separate thing is made up of smaller hypothetically separate things, and is simultaneously part of larger hypothetically separate things. Yes, the *July 24th, 2018 events must be taken as part of a larger actions and plans.*

Positive and negative are related. How much has Nigeria of today progressed and improved her governance index? What is happening with and at our various local government authorities? Nigerians wants restructuring of the working of the federal system such as fiscal federalism. What has happened to the agitation of the people? I am worried and I hope you are. Most of us are only thinking and talking PRESIDENCY. It was *Theodore Roosevelt that once advocated to: "Keep your eyes on the stars, and your feet on the ground." Politics is all about building connections.*

Someone Has Done it Somewhere

Every citizen of this great and beautiful country cannot escape poor leadership and poor governance responsibilities. It will take more than a dedicated president and vice president to make this vision a reality. It will take more than dedicated managers of civil service commission. It will take dedicated citizens, willing to reason and consider the suitability of each candidate that put themselves forward for any elective position. As so many have said, the future is ours – if we have the courage to create it.

When history is said to repeat itself, it is never for good reasons. George Bernard Shaw captured this when he said: *"If history repeats itself, and the unexpected always happens, how incapable must Man be of learning from experience."* The question of whether nations such as Nigeria can learn from her own history or histories of other nations nag policymakers around the world. Part of the problem is that history is handed down through a variety of interpretations that do not reflect reality. But *contemporary history, if genuine presented, can offer policy makers with lessons they can learn from. This is the central message in this chapter. The lessons of Lee Kuan Yew's formidable leadership and success is classic and we can learn from the case study. The late Lee Yew's Singapore was and is a place where multiculturalism and equality are the norm and where racism or ethnic or gender prejudice is just not permitted. The country remarkable performance has less to do with miraculous conditions or luck than with Mr. Lee's model of disciplined, visionary leadership.* Things change peacefully, and the only way they can change peacefully is at the polls and voting for people that can represent us in a way that can enact policy that many people are interested in.

Lee explained in his 1998 memoir "The Singapore Story" that he wanted his country "not just to work but to prosper and flourish." His defining economic policy is arguably uncompromising standards for a universally accessible, top-flight public education system - astutely identifying human capital as Singapore's key competitive advantage - supplemented with rigorous application of meritocracy.

What ensures that Singapore's top officials under late Prime Minister Lee Kuan Yew govern in the interests of the governed, many people have asked. According to one biographical text, "the overall picture is one of an explicit attempt to tie the financial well-being of governors, ministers, administrators and other government appointees with the health of the economy, and hence the public welfare."

Lee Kuan Yew forged a widely admired system of meritocratic, clean, self-reliant, and efficient government and civil service. He has a strong acceptance of the power of culture in shaping policy. *The late prime minister was said to have employed a governance model based on Asian values: the well-being of the collective, the community before the individual. Lee Kuan Yew is known to have constantly stressed the importance of planning for the next lap of development and in thinking in terms of the next big thing to his leadership team. In doing that, leaders must be faster, sharper and more creative in considering their approach to economic governance.*

Some say Singapore's story is sui generis: Something that could only happen in that time and place. But its remarkable performance has less to do with miraculous conditions than with Lee's model of disciplined, visionary leadership. Nigeria aspiring and current leaders should better take pages from Lee Kuan Yew's playbook to address the country current challenges.

Buhari Won a Mandate for Good Governance

That was in 2015. President Buhari once said confidently that Nigeria's problems have more to do with process than structure. And he is right. The Vice President, Professor Yemi Osinbajo said the problem of Nigeria is that the political landscape has been disfigured by poor leadership and bad governance. He is also correct. Nigerians wanted effective government, good governance instead of corruption, opportunity instead of nepotism.

What is good governance? What is good leadership? What is bad leadership? What is poor governance? Let's start with the simple observation that those phrases are fraught with problems, the most pressing of which appears to be a lack of clarity about their actual meaning.

Quality of governance determines the quality of life enjoyed by citizens. Quality of life enjoyed by citizens is determined by better quality public goods and services.

Governance is said to be a multidimensional phenomenon. Governance is the fundamental institutional structure Nigerians [individuals] need to live together peacefully and productively. Tellingly, *Juliet 'Kego must be correct when she commented that "GOVERNANCE is HOW we wield the power/control dynamics (of politics), over the common resources of state, for the common good/overall welfare of the majority of the population (hopefully).* Governance impacts every Nigerians in their day-to-day jobs, whether we work as part of a team, purchase goods or services, manage people, or control budgets. Governance is about raising awareness and sharing information; taking responsibility and providing assurance to stakeholders; and improving our approaches, learning lessons for the future.

Whatever, the actual meaning of good governance, I do not see its arrival in this part of the world until such a time there is a massive reduction in the poverty prevalent among our people and better attitude of the people. What is required for economic growth and development? Good governance is the answer.

Good governance should imply much more than merely the talk of absence of corruption in public finance. What of nepotism, cronyism, injustice, patronage, discrimination or even regulatory policy capture and implementation. Good governance is not just about what we say, what we do, but how we do it, creating an environment that enables positive change and supports strategic approaches to outcomes. A bird cannot fly with one wing only phrase is mostly true. For good governance to be good in Nigeria, it must focus on improving and strengthening of state institutions, processes and structures. If only.

We learnt from the formidable former Prime Minister of Singapore, late Lee Kuan Yew, that good governance is first and foremost about results – production of abundant political goods. That in the end is what matters. It is not a precondition of development but rather the result.

Taking Action to Demand Accountability

The best time to plant a tree was 20 years ago. The second best time is now, a certain Chinese proverb said. The only permission unstoppable people needed are the voice inside them prompting them to move forward. And they moved.

We have allowed many things divide us through the years and it doesn't look better even now. This I know – we aren't going to solve the problems we face quickly, no matter what we do, but we are not going to solve them at all, unless we do this right. Let's make sure that the right people are in the right positions. Let's practice nepotism less and more meritocratic appointments.

And we the people of this great country can achieve the desired good governance if only we can come together, organise and decide to achieve them. *The possibility has reminded me of an Ethiopian proverb: "When spiderwebs combine, they can even tie up a lion."*

Nigerian Leaders are not lazy. Voters Why are you so lazy?

Make no mistake about it. We are reminded every day that the central cause of instability in the country is poor leadership. We are not well-known for truth telling. We simply have very poor quality management and orientation of development policies. President Muhammadu Buhari was right when he declared in his 2015 inaugural speech that, *"daunting as the task may be, it is by no means insurmountable."* Today, the president and Nigerians are trapped between good and evil. Our dreams have turned into a nightmare, and I think it is time to wake up. If, we don't, the nightmare will somehow carry us to destruction. I don't know of any society where nightmares end by themselves.

In politics, serendipity should never be discounted. But then again, neither should persistence, hard work, and unyielding determination. The stars aligned for candidate Muhammadu Buhari in 2015, but that he was there at all to take advantage of them was due to his personal resilience and character. Buhari not only had the desire to be president, but he also possessed the requisite opportunism to realise his ambition. Today he is the president and doesn't need or show a lot of love, as some have argued. He has an air of independence which is misinterpreted as aloofness, but it is a strength and liability which was another of the traits that he carried to the office. Presidents sit in an enviable position. Their office possess – at least theoretically – one third of the national government's power. As chief executives and party leaders, their words and deeds reverberate symbolically and substantially throughout their country and across time. This is a great reason why we must make sure we contribute in deciding who occupies that position. Author *Stephen Skowronek* reminded us that: *"Succeed or fail, presidents are formidable political actors. They are continually remaking our politics, changing the terms of debate and the conditions of maneuver."* Leaders and followers are not separate, very important to remember that.

Buhari and other Nigeria political leaders are not so lazy. It is the people - the voters who are lazy. For instance, President Buhari and elected political leaders did not arrive in their position of responsibility by accident. *They strove and strategised; maneuvered and manipulated; cajoled and charmed all sorts – colleagues, competitors, and we the people. History has proved that the reluctant seldom succeed.* The questions of following ethical and moral directions are open to discussion.

We Must Prevent Lazy Thinking

It is now accepted that new ideas, innovation, and creativity are things we all want to have in our teams, and leaders. However, in reality, our brains are hardwired to prefer information that aligns with what we already know and think. Yes, I am a believer in President Buhari capacity and good intentions and so are millions of Nigerians. I don't expect perfection of him as none can give that. Nigerians made him and Nigerians including associates of him are doing what they can to destroy him and his legacy. A lot of us have been drowned in greed, choked in arrogance, and suffocated by religious bigotry. This is holding the country back. Let us therefore say no to men of little minds. You should not be upset when your thinking is challenged, in fact, you should be grateful. When your thinking is challenged it keeps you from becoming a lazy thinker. Keeping things the same is easy and takes less effort, but it doesn't lead to excellence.

The thinking, for instance, that I am born a south eastern Nigerian; I am therefore an IPOB is hard to accept. I was regarded as such by close powerful associates, and it was very hard to take at the time. If it can happen to me, it can happen to you. As a culture, we tend to criticize what we don't understand. The reason we don't understand it is because we haven't taken the time to know it. If you are in a position of leadership, and if you have credibility and influence, then this message is for you. *To our leaders, work as hard as necessary to prevent lazy thinking. And try not to be what late Senator John McCain once described as, "a human wrecking ball," or "wacko birds."* Whatever you do, remember this, uniformity tends to breed lackluster results. Intuitive prediction, based on biased judgments, borne not of true expertise, very often leads to trouble.

Wake up. Our thoughts have betrayed us. Please, wake up Mr. President! Please wake up Nigerians! The few in the Presidency and various state government houses may have the power, but WE THE PEOPLE in theory has the leadership. The power to lead is in the will of the people. The current nightmares cannot exist without our cooperation and our nightmares will only get worse with each passing administration. For those who have been working to fight for good governance, effective government and human rights for people of all creeds, genders and ethnicities, it is a very dark time. What do we do? We need to speak up more often. *Recently, the current Speaker of the House of Representatives, Hon Yakubu Dogara, stated that for Nigeria to develop and realized her true potentials, the country must undertake restructuring.*

What exactly is the meaning? Refreshing to hear him saying what he said. Our leaders are known to deny knowledge of certain important challenges facing the country. Our leaders including few of our recent presidents are living in denial. It was so even in United States pre First World War era. After the war, Woodrow Wilson publicly poked fun at his own pre-war innocence: *"Let me testify to this, my fellow citizens, I not only did not know it until we got into this war, but I did not believe it when I was told that it was true, that Germany was not the only country that maintained a secret service!"* This is 21st century. Nigeria cannot continue to behave as if we are in pre First World War era.

This book, is saying, no future president or governor or legislator, should take office as uninformed as we have in the recent past and present.

And our culture is full of haters

BUT and the big BUT that add to this book is that I find people are getting lazy and have no idea why they are critiquing certain things and certain people. It is we that decide who among the selected ones become leader, at least in theory. Raise the conversation among your friends, families and networks - make it of value. Move beyond talking about the candidates as people you may like or dislike, and move to talking about the actions they will take as elected officials and how these actions will affect the most vulnerable in the society. Aspiring leaders can't get there without sufficient and committed followers.

Be an energetic thinker, know how you came to the conclusions you came to. Know why, exactly why, you're doing what you're doing. Be prepared to defend everything you do, everything you say and most importantly, everything you think. We must not place too much trust in the wrong people.

In 2014, I was in Copenhagen, Denmark representing the interest of the then Presidential candidate, Muhammadu Buhari in an open debate event tagged: *"Nigeria at Crossroad"* as part of 2015 general election campaign. My case then was that with Muhammadu Buhari at the helm of affairs, Nigeria will get "creativity in leadership, better security for life and property, willingness to learn from experiences elsewhere, readiness to implement good ideas quickly and decisively through an efficient public service." That was 2014/2015. This is NOW. Any regrets, of course not. It is said that in free society, some are guilty, but all are responsible.

This is a kind of condition where former Princeton psychologist Daniel Kahneman, the only non-economist to be awarded the Nobel Prize in economics so far, describes in his 2011 book, *Thinking Fast and Slow: "it is wrong to blame anyone for failing to forecast accurately in an unpredictable world, however, it seems fair to blame professionals for believing they can succeed in an impossible task."* It is as simple as that. It wasn't my fault who supported him if he failed to be consistent in his integrity credentials.

It is time that the country leaders set out to do something concrete and not just focus on the trappings of statesmanship. In my journey for this book, I have come to admire late Lee Kuan Yew, Singapore's first prime minister abundantly. *If you are a current political leader or potential future leader in Nigeria, Lee Kuan Yew, must have had you in mind when he said: "anyone who thinks he is a statesman needs to see a psychiatrist."* Is Lee Kuan Yew perfect? No. None of us will ever be perfect, but he proved during his time to be self-aware and coachable. You must not destroy what you don't understand. Self-awareness gives us power!

Way Forward

Hello present and future voters, ask yourself before you decide on whom to support and vote for, does that present and future leader have belief in the supremacy of the quality of human capital? Does that person understand the meet the needs of the present without compromising the ability of future generations to meet their own needs. Political leadership matters, and so does quality civil service. Political parties should put considerable effort in their recruitment of political talent. History has shown that not every willing individual has the capacity.

What happens next is up to you. Personal responsibility is an important key factor. Former Vice President Atiku Abubakar is probably correct when he said: human actors are largely responsible for the current state of affairs that makes the realization of good governance difficult in Nigeria.

Don't be afraid. It is 'we the people' that can make democratic elections enervate or energise effective government and good governance. There is no democratic paradise, no easy way out. Going forward, we must accept the saying that a dying mule kicks the hardest. Sometimes, it kicks very hard indeed. Obstacles are often smaller than they appear. *Leaders should know that people are bigger than obstacles. Good leaders make sound decisions. It must not always as it is currently is, depend on political necessity.*

Each at their own time, each at their own pace, each in their own way. Coming out is a process, a journey, not a race. Unlike most journeys, there is no one destination in mind, only a direction. Keep on. When you stray, or slow down, don't be afraid to ask advice or direction. Your journey is yours alone, and regardless of where you end up, or when, don't let anyone else plan the trip.

Steve Basile

3

Voter's Education Need More Wave Makers

Nigeria is blessed with both human resources and natural resources
but the country continued to bedevilled with Leadership woes
hampering its development.

Until Nigerian leadership space is structured to reward merit, the
wise will continue to give up his rights to the uninformed, with the
blind attempting to lead the sighted, and the unskilled
directing the skilled. Chaos!
Miriam Yakubu Ikunaiye

NIGERIA HAS A DEMOCRACY PROBLEM. The crisis of poor governance has been building for decades. Levers of power are not controlled by the people. Free and fair elections are the cornerstone of our kind of democracy, and it has become clear that it has not worked in Nigeria. Why is not happening in Nigeria? Some have attributed to *"truth decay," (a phrase, I have borrowed from RAND CORPORATION report)* defined as an increasing disagreement about facts and analytical interpretations of facts and data; a blurring of the line between opinion and fact; an increase in the relative volume, and resulting influence, of opinion and personal experience over fact; and lowered trust in formerly respected sources of factual information.

What did we learn from the July 24th 2018 episode in the Senate and House of Representatives? THE BEST WORDS to describe politics in Nigeria are fragmentation and disarray. Being a politician is like being the richest man in town–everyone wants to get close to you in order to ask for favors. We have all been disenfranchised. It's time to think the unthinkable. As we saw in 2015, the feeling that power is not in their hands made the citizens more, not less, to entrust their fate to President Buhari, who promises to smash the system - airy promises. What we read on the dailies and saw on the electronic news media was not exactly what was happening. There is massive lack of shared leadership responsibilities in Nigeria.

Want To Change the Face Of Politics in Nigeria?

Voter's education must be the top priority of every person that wants good results from development and peace in Nigeria. Hello Mr. President, continual communications from YOU and not from twisted mouths, helps the people understand where they fit in the big picture, and helps them prioritize tasks to line up with your administration's greater mission. You could stumble and stutter over your ideas, but if people saw you speaking consistently to the things you truly believed, and felt that you truly understand them and respected their views, you were far more likely to make the vital connection that would attract them to your vision even further. We must build trust when times get tough and things are tough NOW. We must change the practice of government where a rarefied few represent the needs of the many.

Are you willing to educate your fellow voters?

Drop a pebble in the stillest of ponds and you will create ripples all over the surface. I see you, reading this page, as a leader. Though leaders are responsible for maintaining peace, it is also their job to occasionally be the architects of plans that disrupt status quo and complacency. The first step toward enacting change is to strategically inform a few of the right people.

Good voter education has components that might seem obvious to you, but they may not be obvious to someone who has never voted before or who is reluctant to participate. The ripples will naturally and organically emanate from the surface to touch everyone that needs to be in the know. And the waves you generate will create valuable soundings.

What is at stake? Everyone has issues that are a priority to them. For many young and 'lazy' people, better job prospects are at the top. Others are mostly concerned about getting a good and affordable education. For the whole nation, it's mostly about effective government and good governance. Effective government and good governance needed to guarantee better job prospects, good and affordable education and security of life can only be accomplished by having the right people at the right positions. It is therefore very important that voters think, however superficially, about the major parties and individual candidates they support. It is morally wrong for political parties to only think about individuals who can help them win elections. Persons who can govern or legislate well should be the ultimate aims of candidate selection options.

Sadly, it is not happening. Our politicians must remember that cynicism breeds cynicism. It is essential that our political parties select candidates, who are at least coachable. A *person who is coachable not only responds well when given feedback, they ask for feedback. They view the input from others as a valuable.*

Cultures are long-lasting; they have evolved over centuries and they change slowly. In his book *The Secret of Our Success, Joseph Henrich of Harvard University* writes that when politicians design new policies, they inevitably import their own assumptions about human nature, often rooted in Enlightenment philosophies. He points out that as we have seen from the sad experience of transplanting Western institutions to countries that have different incentives and standards for judging and punishing people, the new norms need to fit in with people's social norms, informal institutions and cultural psychology. People are selective social learners, *Henrich warns, which means that they do not change their habits purely based on "the facts" or "education"; rather, they copy the behaviour of influential people in their social circles.*

People are more likely to learn from those whose prestige, success, sex, dialect and ethnicity they consider important. Let each one of us represent that people! Just as we know that behind every successful leader lie a capable team and many followers, behind all good leadership is good governance.

Doing a good job isn't enough; present and future leaders must be culturally astute. People that fall in love with the positions and not the responsibilities are poor leaders as they think with their heart. They tend not to be objective, they often times overlook critical items, pad their decisions with denial and hope. Our country is going down. We all must focus on practicing servant leadership principles of values, learning, teaching, growth, and community.

Change in social policies depends on the entire society. Or, as Henrich puts it, change depends on the expansion of the collective brain, which in turn depends on openness to discussing issues and ideas. So, what do we do as a society? Perhaps, practice makes perfect. Democracy is supposed to enact the will of the people. But what if the people have no clue what they're doing? Paraphrasing political scientist Philip Converse, the two simplest truths about the distribution of political information in moderate electorates are that the mean is low and variance is high. In other words, most people know nothing, some know less than nothing (that is, they are systematically mistaken rather than just ignorant), and some know a great deal. The uninformed electorates will always greatly outnumber the informed. When given a choice, a lot of uninformed people chooses to choose badly. The more electorates we can move to informed, the more the quality of our candidates would be.

Hello Nigerians, we must all times chase perfection. As Vince Lombardi loudly stated, *"Perfection is not attainable, but if we chase perfection we can catch excellence."* And I believe that. Beliefs underlie every single thing we do, both individually and organisationally. Beliefs are like the root system of our lives. The reason to write this book could not be more obvious. The Hawaiians say, *"Never turn your back on the ocean."* This means; don't turn your back to energy, don't be arrogant and think you are more powerful than the sea. You aren't. To me, it also means that we must each tell the truth and repair what is in disrepair and breakdown and recreate what is old and outdated. It is asking a lot. It's asking for everything from every citizen of our country.

Researching all the past presidents and selected state governors, I have come to accept that past patterns do not determine the future, but they do clarify the stakes of the game. As we have had in our past elections, when the old order loses political purchase, the attractions of the loner-as-leader shine brightly. But such presidents or governors are never been able to reorder national or state affairs. Once in office, they appear incompetent and in over their heads.

What Leaders of today and tomorrow Need to
Navigate Waves

4

Redefining How You Lead:
What Nigerians Said They Want

As fleeting as power is, it will always be the prized possession of the masses. No matter how long it goes missing, it must always return to the people. What we the people then decide to do with it, is up to us!
Osasu Igbinedion

Criticism may not be agreeable, but it is necessary. It fulfills the same function as pain in the human body; it calls attention to the development of an unhealthy state of things. If it is heeded in time, danger may be averted; if it is suppressed, a fatal distemper may develop.
Winston Churchill

OUR ENVIRONMENT IS WICKED TO THE CORE and life is suffering. That's clear. And this is irrefutable truth. Majority of Nigerians are both power-poor and income-poor. From the beginning, we have been conditioned to believe certain things, and these beliefs go deep into the roots of our identity, and they affect our sense of who we are. *North East, North West, North Central, South South, South West or South East* we all have our demons and nightmares. Once we have accepted the belief systems we are born into, they lure us into a particular nightmare. We are confined to them and held by them and from all indications; we end up passing them on! There is a work here to be done - and it is the truth. Let's hear what our people have to say. As Maya Angelou said, *the greatest burden to bear is that of an untold story in your heart.* The shaping of minds is a more decisive and lasting form of domination than the submission of bodies by intimidation or violence.

The problem with Nigeria democracy is voters. Yes Voter behaviour is erratic and incoherent. Most people pay little attention to qualification of elective office candidates; when they vote if they vote at all they do so irrationally and for contradictory reasons!

Ultimately the question of nature of leaders for inclusive institutions, sustained economic growth and capabilities and freedoms in Nigeria – today and tomorrow is what this book is written to answer. And we will. And Nigerians thinks they have the answers and this book transcreate the personal characteristics that Nigerians said they are looking for in their future leaders. Even though most assumes that a leader can get anything done; leadership depends on the circumstance.

There is no Myers-Briggs test for successful presidents or governors or senators or our town union elected officials. On that Election Day, voters must take a leap. But maybe the characteristics listed in this chapter and discussed in the rest of oncoming chapters would help us see a little more clearly where we should land.

What do we do?

The Nigerian general election of 2015 and actions of the current President Buhari administration confirmed the old adage that nothing is carved in stone. At least not in politics and not in most things relating to Nigeria. WE have to be unstoppable to be successful. In this environment, constant change is the new normal. You are in control of you. And that's what you're going to do. But I accept that every individual is a conscious or unconscious follower of some influential philosopher. Very few people will give you the truth. Completely own it when you screw up and our political leaders are not doing that. We must be succinctly opposed to leaders who treat essentially every figure opposed to them as hopelessly corrupt and not working for the benefit of the people. Populism is not always correct. Populists are the elite and pretend they have the answers and this is why right or left wing populism is the greatest danger to democracy as people are being misled.

What our politician should be basing their politics on is; how is your family doing? But none of them including the current leaders are doing that! The truth that we perceive about most of them is subjective and can be wrong. The populists among our leaders are lazy and busy suggesting simple solutions for often very complicated problems.

In 2018 Nigeria, wrath of justice is becoming more blind and pigheaded silence is becoming normal. It is not right. Leaders and associates are getting crushed by privileges. Privilege can become a catalyst for failure. The most dangerous thing is the manipulation of the truth and that is the greatest threat to our democracy.

Nigerians are not gradualism enthusiasts, and rightly so. We have endured so much that gradualism would not only be misguided but risky in most of our communities.

NOW, one thing is certain; we all need to take responsibility for the future of Nigeria. We need to come together and make our country great. *Nigerians are in love with core conservative values of personal responsibility, self-reliance, restrained government, shared community, and the moral authority of tradition. Nigerians are capable people.* It was Robert Schuller who once wrote … *let your hopes, not your hurts, shape your future.* Nigerians are desperate for leaders with deliberate collegial temperament leadership philosophy and who understand the notion of fiscal federalism. Very important – as commonly said there can be wisdom from the camp of the second wife. Opposition matters!

Redefining How You Lead

It's time to redefine leadership for the new world we are living in. What worked in the past isn't going to work in the future. All of us as leaders need to start demanding more of ourselves.

One obvious issue is a lack of transparency in Nigeria politics is how merit is measured. Think about it. This chapter is a summary of the transcreated views of so many Nigerians. The message is this: l*et this book be your reference in that next argument at the dinner table or debate on social media or any productive hangout on the state of our country or communities.* It is said that the greatest improvement that we ever had is when we had more challenging times. This is definitely challenging times in Nigeria.

What follows are the distinct but interconnected trans-created qualities Nigerians are looking for in their leaders. Taken together, these qualities are meant to paint a picture of a process for the systematic pursuit of truth and excellence and for the rewards that accompany this pursuit. Having traits that work and wanted by the people is essential for getting what we want out of our institutions.

Nepotism is morally wrong: Leadership should be focused on extending the ladder of opportunity for everyone. Can leaders you support recognise baloney when it comes from their staff or supporters? Do they know how to hire a good team? Nigerians said they need leaders that would bring people together. That brings diversity to a common cause. What you aim at determines what you see.

Concerned about the ability to bring change and care for its impact on people: The job of a leader is to find the common good, not to protect their own tribe. Leaders must be concerned with the impact his or her actions have on all the people not some people. We are not going to arrive at mutual respect, which is where we solve common problems, if we wrap ourselves in an ideological, social or intellectual bubble. But for us to move forward, to keep moving and moving forward, we have to do it together – all together. Nigerians has to fight our ancestral mindset.

Management ability: Is the candidate focused enough to follow an overarching vision, but nimble enough to tweak that vision when real-world events intervene? Can they admit mistakes and learn from them? Can they sift through complex ideas? Can they recognize baloney when it comes from their staff or supporters? Do they know how to hire a good team? Critical thinking and problem solving are needed in today's work environment that is moving at a faster pace than ever.

People follow leaders into the unknown only when there is a foundation of trust. Trust is a big word, one we use a lot, and that touches so many different areas of life, from love to politics. And that trust is born out of personal incorruptibility and moral authority on the part of leaders. In order to provide the foundation for good governance, Nigeria needs to build up its social and cross-cultural capital. Social capital greatly involves the trust that the citizens have on the leaders, as well as trust in each other. Leaders can only be effective if there's a deep sense of trust between the institutions they lead and its people.

Leader at any level of government must be an effective communicator. You must be willing and able to speak to the people. Delegation is important but Nigerians as does want to hear directly from their leader as often as possible. In doing that, remember, a good speech must be truthful. It must not pander to the emotions. It must take into account the citizen's mood and guide their passions and imagination, while using the words of the common man. However there are some particular behaviors that make people see a potential leader as embodying the charisma. These include having a compelling vision and communicating it clearly and often; being proactive and change-oriented; appealing to followers' personal values; conveying optimism about future possibilities; and treating followers as human beings rather than cynically and manipulatively. The candidate must be able to constantly and consistently communicate visions in ways that can tackle tough challenges. Nigeria future leaders must have the capacity to lead conversations about what's essential and what's not. Nigerians want leaders who speak with clarity.

Relatedness is highly valuable. In our interconnected and interdependent world, relationships matter more than ever. Obviously, elective politicians or appointees must relate to a diverse public. President Olusegun Obasanjo was particularly effective in social relations, which supporters attributed to his outgoing personality and natural political skills, but opponents saw as manipulative and deceptive. President Buhari appears to be getting along well with groups especially those who had political dispositions and beliefs similar to his. One of them is definitely doing less in situations in which inquisitiveness, incisiveness, sophisticated discussion, and educated explanations are expected. It is also possible that President Obasanjo most times allowed his personal needs and anxieties affect his political and policy decisions more than you can say of President Buhari. Relatedness trumps responsibility, accountability. How we relate to ourselves and others is central to creating and maintaining effective and valuable systems.

Leaders of the future need to have the stomach for conflict and uncertainty - among their people and within themselves. Yes conflict is dangerous: It can damage relationships. It can threaten friendships. But conflict is the primary engine of creativity and innovation. People don't learn by staring into a mirror; people learn by encountering difference. There is no doubt that the current federal government lead by President Muhammadu Buhari has the stomach for conflict and uncertainty. Nevertheless, you wouldl be right if you asked if the creativity and innovation have followed.

Malleability is a necessary quality in a leader. Constancy has a nice romantic ring to it, but does anyone want a leader who sets a course and then refuses to change it no matter what? A competent leader is expected to understand that there is a sequence to implementing visions. He should orbit around the mission rather than around his or her ego. Success or failure of any leader can be measured in his or her ability to anticipate future trends, ability to revise or change course where required and openness to learning from lessons learnt elsewhere. Effective leaders adapt by showing what can be done regardless of the complications or restrictions placed upon them.

Character | Authenticity | Dignity | Accountability. Integrity is taken here to mean the capacity to remain true to one's ideals, values, and beliefs. Integrity provides an ethical framework for understanding and making judgments within a larger social context. Leaders who lack integrity tend to be driven by their own self-interests, which they often rationalize in terms of the public good. The future leader must be trusted with capacity to follow through on promises. The danger comes when conditions change, when new issues arise, the public mood shifts, but the leader continue to pursue old policies and the beliefs that underlie them, as nothing had changed. Leaders of the present and future must be accountable and willing to hold others accountable.

Must have sense of optimism | ambition |vision | bold | resilience– the future leaders must have capacity to demonstrate sense of belief in self and others, is absolutely essential for leaders. We can't have leaders who continue to feed the depression, feed the anxiety. How they handle this opportunity comes down to preparation, persistence, and passion. Desire drives success, passion carries the day. These attributes are each unique and essential, yet they are all interdependent. They share a great deal in common, yet their distinctions matter.

Open-mindedness yet assertiveness or straightforwardness – future leaders need to collaborate and work with other people, but also need to have the ability to be self-directed and self-controlled in own thinking and not always be influenced by fads or whim or fancy, because then it is possible to get off course too often from what's really important to them.

Capacity to learn - Yes we want Nigeria to move forward. Yes we can. First thing first! Let's make a commitment that all individuals to be considered for an elective position must have capacity to learn. If they are, it becomes possible to expect that all political appointees will be like them. It is essential to ask the question on learn-ability. Why? Often things do not go as planned. If presidents find that their beliefs need to be modified and their operating style adjusted, they must do so in a way that does not undermine their authenticity, credibility, and strength of character. In today's rapidly changing world, it's not what people already know but how quickly they can learn that matters.

Leaders need a high level of self-awareness and emotional intelligence. Self-awareness is the meta-skill of the 21st century. The qualities most critical for business and leadership success today—things like emotional intelligence, empathy, influence, persuasion, communication, and collaboration—all stem from self-awareness. Nigerians wants future leaders who don't show features of inactive, sluggish, slow moving or plodding on both thoughts and actions.

Real leaders have accountability, fairness, inclusivity in abundance. They don't blame others, don't claim credit for the success of their team, but always accept responsibility for failures that occur on their watch. Most of all, leaders are accountable to their team. Leaders not accountable to their people will eventually be held accountable by their people. The role of leader is a multifaceted one, for one must be able to persuade others, make decisions, resolve conflicts, and effectively regulate oneself. An effective leader had to foster an illusion of fairness, not just for tough times but all times. People want to know leaders care about them as people, not just as voters. It's about treating our people as they'd like to be treated – and for that, leaders need to genuinely know who they are and what matters to them in their lives. Anyone can lead well when conditions are favorable, but it is your conduct in times of adversity that distinguishes you as an excellent leader.

A big grievance Nigerians bring about their leaders on a consistent basis is that most leaders talk "at" them, instead of listening to them. When leaders listen, they can prepare much better. It amazes me how many leaders like to listen to themselves rather than those they serve. You can't lead if you don't listen. As a leader, listening allows you to prepare more intently and solve for things that you otherwise couldn't if you were only listening to yourself.

Nigerians said Lack of Past Elective Position Experience is Not a Show Stopper. They do want unnecessary political promises. Swagger is not a correct virtue. Nigerians want simple truth. We have seen lately that what a politician 'says' is unimportant. However, what you said and what you do are both very important. Only what one intends is important. Nigerians lie about lying. We make up unworkable moral rules like it's OK to lie with silence, but not with false statements. Lying is distorting or concealing the truth. We all do both. We say things we know aren't exactly true or aren't the whole truth.

You can't led without Emotional Courage

According to Peter Bregman, the critical challenge of leadership is mostly the challenge of emotional courage. This is the courage to care about people, to empathise or sympathise with others. It means speaking up when others are not and remaining steadfast, grounded and measured in the face of uncertainty. It means responding productively to political opposition and challenges facing our communities.

Nigerians are encouraging all political parties fielding candidates in any election to set in motion a system where candidates must complete a psychological test with as many questions as possible and face-to-face interviews for clinical assessment. Non-disclosure Doctors should examine childhood and family life, educational background, experience with community service, sex psychology history, marriage habits, social activities, health, work experience, finances, life philosophy and political motivation. In this exercise, past performance in grass-roots work should be given higher priority than the psychological test. The role of the commission would end with the issuing of a status statement. Acting on that information - or ignoring or disparaging it - would be up to the people before an election and the elected legislators afterward.

The extent of overlap of the listed traits is telling. I know it is a tough list and to find a single candidate with the qualities and able to it all would be unrealistic and impossible. However, that should not stop us from exploring the possible.

The traits connect leader's values to their abilities and skills. It is accepted that while values or the deep-seated beliefs that motivate behaviours and abilities or ways of thinking and behaving are unlikely to change much, most skills can be acquired in a limited amount of time.

Going Forward

This book is about taking action to change the country for the better. Politics involves institutions and systems of norms and principles of power management, ideally designed and set in motion for the common good. President Buhari once said: I belong to everyone … I belong to no one. Who else can say that in Nigeria and how true is that! Personality is said to involves intra-individual systems and self-regulatory mechanisms that guide people toward achieving individual and collective goals, while providing coherence and continuity in behavioral patterns and a sense of personality identity cross different setting.

The chapters that follow are something more than separate essays and something less than the chapters of a book. They develop a point of view cumulatively rather than an argument sequentially. Each takes up an issue or two broached in this chapter and elaborated both politically and theoretically. And address either directly or indirectly the relationship among democratic politics and political education. Ultimately, what skills, values and approaches should underpin the coherent and successful present-day leaders are the objectives in this book.

5

Character | Authenticity | Dignity | Accountability

The credit belongs to the man who is actually in the arena -
whose face is marred by dust and sweat and blood...who knows
the great enthusiasms, the great devotions - and spends himself
in a worthy cause - who at best if he wins knows the thrills of
high achievement - and if he fails at least fails while daring
greatly - so that his place shall never be with those cold and
timid souls who know neither victory or defeat.
Theodore Roosevelt

Character is the distinctive behavioural pattern of a person. It is
critical to know that character speaks. Your character makes
statements whether you are aware or not, and the statement of
your character is louder than the utterance of your speech.
Paul Enenche

WHEN LOOKING INTO TRAITS, characteristics and capabilities that each candidate must be assessed on, it's good to look deeply into each candidate's values or deep beliefs that guide behaviour. And that is the main focus of this chapter.

Trust is collapsing in Nigeria. Who can we trust is one of the most pressing issues that we face in our institutions? Sometimes, it is not a lack of trust but rather a case of placing too much trust in the wrong people, institutions and places. It is that bad that my optimism for the future of the country comes with big caveats. You must be very conscious of who is filling the vacuum and what their intentions are. Truth itself feels uncertain. We love telling lies and believing lies. There is a lot of chaos and uncertainty in the country. And there is absolutely no need for the continuous leadership blame game going on from one administration to another. The presidency or the state governorship is a place where a man or woman has agreed to take on the responsibility with huge possible failures. Lately, so much of our politics and government, have devolved into a toxic fog of moneyed interests, self-interest, celebrity, cynicism, hunger for power, superficial sound bites, hidden agendas, and hypocrisy.

Nigerians are saying to our political leaders, you need something special: *they are called character - authenticity, trustworthy, dignity, and accountability.* The focus on character and accountability in the next election cycle is a strong and positive sign that Nigerians want, and will demand, fundamental change in the operation of our government. It is encouraging that this quest for radical change is largely led by educated employed and unemployed youth and university students who have suffered some of the worst effects of the dysfunction of our political institutions, and who will shape the future landscape of our political life.

Who Are You?

Character is at the heart of being an effective leader. It represents who you are and what you stand for. Character is ultimately defined by those values or deep beliefs that guide behaviour. The best leaders of character define and communicate those values, then bring them to life through living them, and reward others who live them. Character and its derivatives are essentially products of years of development. They are a compilation of life's experiences and all of which are difficult to undo while the today and tomorrow uncertain circumstances requires a mobile person. Thus, a person of the highest moral character must also possess learning intelligence ability to be an effective leader. *Character encompasses the virtues of drive, authenticity, collaboration, humility, humanity, integrity, courage, temperance, accountability, transcendence, justice, judgement - plus commitment.*

Authenticity is becoming a huge buzzword in our political scene and will obviously play a big part in the next election cycle and rightly so. Depending on whom your sources are: Muhammadu Buhari and

Goodluck Jonathan are both lauded for it. Taking stock of a candidate's character should play a critical role in all our elections. Much has been made of the 'authenticity' of the respective candidates – because we live in times where, more than ever, we don't trust leaders. But "authenticity," standing alone, tells us nothing about whether a person has the integrity and requisite leadership qualities to be a result-oriented president or governor or legislator. We have to be particularly attuned to perception versus reality when we view a politician as "authentic."

While gauging authenticity is difficult, the more fundamental problem is that authenticity is a woefully inadequate barometer of virtue or ability. The question should not be whether someone is authentic, but rather who is he or she "authentically" like. *You can be authentically confident, tough, honest, ethical, restrained, and compassionate. Or you can be an authentic corrupt, an authentic religionist, an authentic bully, or an authentic fool.* In addition, simply trying to assess whether someone is "authentic" is not going to do the trick. Policy positions of the person are critically important. Although without more, they can be as ephemeral as wind direction. Accordingly, transformational leadership skills to motivate its team to be effective and efficient and the commitment to carry the policy positions forward are equally significant. So, is being authentic enough to be a leader? And my answer is NO!

How About Restrained Emotion?

There's no question that composure under daily killings and other devastations happening in our country is an essential quality in a leader, but excessive calm can be too much of a good thing. Composure is a big strength, but if you never show any negative emotion, especially in a crisis or in response to bad news, people won't see you as authentic and nobody trusts a phony. Believe me, President Buhari reputation is suffering massively over this. The president's disconcerting patterns related to calmness require explanation.

Accountability shows Responsibility and Acceptance to own one's Actions

Culture of entitlement is a common phrase employed in describing various leaders of our governments over the years. As citizens, we have neglected the responsibility to hold leaders accountable. And most political leaders surrounded themselves with loyalists with no sense of accountability or responsibility. Who among all the leadership candidates you know is ready to accept that accountability and ethics in government have to stem from conviction, not from rules. Either you have integrity or you don't.

Leading through accountability is essential for our survival as a nation. Accountability shows not only responsibility, but acceptance to own one's actions and to lead by example. Genuine leaders are those who are prepared to accept accountability and personal ownership. And accountability is not about blame. Rather, it is about addressing what went wrong and correcting it. *Lazy leaders and not lazy youth must keep in mind that it is easy to focus on who failed rather than focus on the processes and structures that broke down or caused the failure.* Genuine leaders take disciplinary action when part of the problem does involve people's failure.

Action always beats inaction. We must remember that there are no straight lines in the universe. Life doesn't travel in perfectly straight lines. It moves more like a winding river. More often than not, you can only see to the next bend, and only when you reach that next turn can you see more. Political leadership transformed Singapore. Leadership can transform Nigeria if only we elect and appoint well.

The philosopher William Kingdon Clifford wrote an essay titled: The Ethics of Belief, in which he argued: *"It is wrong always, everywhere, and for anyone to believe anything on insufficient evidence."* Have any of the leadership candidates you are considering voting for proved themselves either from their past productivity or sign of ability to learn?

No Integrity is Unquestionable

Who is your leadership candidate? Their constituencies may be on the south, or the east, or the west, or the northern region, but they live in Nigeria and have served in any previous Nigeria government. How much true are his or her intentions? Is he or she someone you can look up? Or could it be, the more you look, the less you probably see. If we are concerned at all about our country and its future, we must pay attention to the election and use our votes and support wisely. As a voter, it is not easy to judge from a distance. Leading through integrity means seeking the truth and changing our positions when we gain better perspective. We must be aware of leaders perceived to have integrity but who are not keen to accept the consequences of speaking and defending the truth.

As was in the past federal government administrations, so it is probably in the present one. Time will tell. Contrary to the pristine image that democratic institutions such as presidency, legislative houses promote, the institutions are plagued by discord between the communities and the leaders, a lack of transparency. Do we have values? So the question in the coming elections should not be who is going to lead us, but what are our standards for being led? In short, if you want leadership with integrity, then stop trusting people who lie for our own good. If people are lying on your behalf and you are not speaking up against the lies, then you too is a big liar.

Going Forward

There is way for a better future; if we are keen on the better way. Timing is everything in political and economic growth and transformation. Look for real and not perceived integrity, strong character, authenticity, enthusiasm, confidence, creativity, humility, dignity, patience and accountability from each of the leadership candidates. Many of Nigerians youth and elderly are beginning to see it that way. They're losing hope with each week. But I tell them it's the best possible time to be in the resistance. And I am telling you here now. *Only during times of* *darkness can you see the stars, the late Martin Luther King once said.*

Nigerians want leaders. Not ideologues. Not people whose life experiences have been so narrow that they've been able to maintain the purity of their youthful ideals. I think there's a glorious rainbow that beckons those with the spirit of adventure. Rainbow is not restricted to eastern or western point. Get my drift? There can be rich findings at the end of that rainbow. Have courage and follow that rainbow and ride it. I encourage us to inspect what we expect from each candidate and endeavour to expect what we have inspected. We must learn to follow up. Yes follow up and follow up.

The ultimate test of the value of a political system at presidential or gubernatorial level is whether it helps the society establish conditions that improve the standard of living for the majority of its people.

It is a known fact, that, when you dare aspire upward, you reveal the inadequacy of the present and the promise of the future. Sometimes, you have the feeling that, what we have in our various institutions are not what the country was created to be or have. The power has started dictating the values more than the values the power. Both the nature of power and the way power gets deployed need changes!

6

Nigerians Says NEPOTISM is Morally Wrong

Many people are always saying the Presidency is too big a job for any
one man. When I hear this assertion, I always try to point out that a
single man must make the final decisions that affect the whole, but
that proper organization brings to him only the questions and
problems on which his decisions are needed. His own job is to be
mentally prepared to make those decisions and then to be supported
by an organization that will make sure they are carried out.
Dwight D. Eisenhower

There has been a great noise made about removals. ... It is rotation in
office that will perpetuate our liberty.
Andrew Jackson

HAVE WE CREATED THE MOST UNITARY, overpowered,
overburdened executive in our Presidency? Many recent headlines have
brought attention to accusations that our presidency and various state
government houses are practicing nepotism. Presidential nepotism is
almost as old as the presidency itself. For better or worse, it is probably
our tradition and it brings ethical issues. Nepotism is the root cause of
public-sector problems. *"A presidential cabinet that looks like Nigeria
would not be hard to achieve. A gender-parity cabinet is doable"*
Proneness to promoting undeserving family members should be
challenged and voters should be careful of such a leader. The results –
mediocrity steeped in corruption and poverty of the mind and the team.
It feels everywhere. It's not just present but past but Nigerians are asking
for a different tomorrow! Nepotism is corruption.

Yes, taking advantage of family connections doesn't necessarily
amount to nepotism but it is morally wrong and should be regarded as
dent to such leader's character and competence. It's a flaw in our
structure going back to the beginning but it is becoming worse. *As any
historian would say, scale matters.* If nepotism becomes widespread; the

human potential of societies will be lost. Not aware is not leadership. We support delegating but not abdicating.

WE CAN do BETTER

I researched but didn't see any written policy asking people to please abide by the rules of common sense. You will never find it anywhere, because otherwise there would be no such thing as common sense. Let's do something about the practice of nepotism. Voters should whack such leaders that seem to find value in such act. The nepotism in politics has created more inequality in our society and that inequality reinforces the nepotism in politics. This is why we need only ethical persons in leadership positions. It's not going to happen naturally.

We ask all head of government to approached governance affairs with a simple principle, *"to ask nothing that is not clearly right, and to submit to nothing that is wrong."* Hello Nigerians, it is time to raise our standards and expectations from our leaders. It is the minimum expected of the citizens. *Love him or hate, he said what he understands and tries to keep to his promises. It was President Donald Trump that said, "If the righteous many do not confront the wicked few, then evil will triumph. When decent people and nations become bystanders to history, the forces of destruction only gather power and strength."*

It's so much more complicated to be President now than it was in 2011 or 1999. President Buhari has faced more issues than any other Nigeria presidents. It's not only that the issues themselves are more complicated—there's so many of them and there are so many interdependencies between them. The proliferation of issues creates interconnections that are hard to see and understand.

To succeed in creating the future, we must also excel in letting go of the past: selectively forgetting practices and attitudes that stand in the way of the new future. How do we know what to cut? It's important to distinguish between our roots and the beliefs we can get rid of. If we cut a tree's roots, the tree dies. Roots, like dedication to core purpose and vision, have timeless value and leaders need to preserve and nourish them. In the long term, the idea of nepotism does more harm than good. *It is dreadful to leave out someone on the basis of "state of origin and religion," and not on merit.*

Remember that when next you think of who next to support for presidency, governorship and legislative positions. The great Lee Kwan Yew said: "Without high quality leadership, a country cannot become great." Let's vote ONLY high quality candidates. Nigeria must be great!

Head of Government Must Be Ready to Build Governing Team

Leaders must also understand and manage the change process, and address problems quickly as they arise. People form opinions pretty quickly, and these opinions tend to be sticky. When in doubt, over-communicate! Preparing to take over the presidency of the Federal Republic of Nigeria or Lagos State Government is highly complex and extremely important. Done well, it will set up a new administration for success; done poorly, it will make it difficult for a new administration to recover. It has happened before and Nigerians are saying never again.

In the 1972 dramatic film *The Candidate,* a dazed U.S. Senator-elect Bill McKay learns he has won a hard-fought election. Turning to his campaign manager, he asks, "So … what do we do now?"

Planning to govern must never be an afterthought. This classic fictional scene highlights the real-life difficulty of preparing to govern in the midst of campaigning, and the void that is created if planning does not take place. Candidates cannot wait until after the election to begin thinking about how they will organize and prepare to deal with such emergencies or the demanding day-to-day requirements of governing. This work must begin in the midst of the presidential or governorship campaign so the new administration will be ready to govern and be prepared for any possibility - on day one.

Nigerians are saying NO to future leaders behaving as atrocious saints. Nigerians are asking for leaders capable of promoting and executing the idea that anyone can succeed through hard work and natural ability, rather than through unearned power and privilege. Our government at most levels appears to be busy but the adage said: *being busy does not always mean real work.* The object of all work is production or accomplishment. Seeming to do is not nothing. High standards are great (and necessary) when you're a leader. But it becomes a problem when having high standards translates into lack of flexibility when faced with a forced detour. That helps no one.

You hired a clone. Saying You are Fired is NOT a Weakness

It is difficult to know who is serving in the public interest if government service is a personal privilege. People in Nigeria government working exclusively for personal privilege are so many and it is one basic reason for continual practices in partiality syndrome.

Think of it, a key measure of the president or governor, as leader of a government business is their capacity to select their team or cabinet. This obviously is very important, if the leader's visions are to be properly executed. While leaders must have vision, they need more. Vision usually has exclusive reference to the future. President's team, or Governor's team, or wife of the president's team must understand the times and know what to do if they are properly staffed. *In one passage, the Bible talks about the soldiers in King David's army. About the men of Issachar, it says they "understood the times and knew what Israel should do" (1 Chronicles 12:32).* This is what I mean by insight. Leaders need wisdom and discernment for the present.

Such wisdom are so difficult to come from YES men and women of yesterday who are now in position of authority advising the leader. If honest truth be said, which should be a standard operating nationwide, looking at the present presidential team, it appears there is a lack of adherence to the legal maxim that "he who comes to equity must come with clean hands." The president and all governors must ensure that the officers' selection process is initiated and executed in accord with standard procedures.

I am very motivated by words credited to *former US President, Dwight Eisenhower,* used on the occasion of accepting the nomination of the Republican National Convention in 1956. He was reported to have said:

Such wisdom are so difficult to come from YES men and women of yesterday who are now in position of authority advising the leader. If honest truth be said, which should be a standard operating nationwide, looking at the present presidential team, it appears there is a lack of adherence to the legal maxim that "he who comes to equity must come with clean hands." The president and all governors must ensure that the officers' selection process is initiated and executed in accord with standard procedures.

I am very motivated by words credited to *former US President, Dwight Eisenhower,* used on the occasion of accepting the nomination of the Republican National Convention in 1956. He was reported to have said: *"One of my predecessors is said to have observed that in making his decisions he had to operate like a football quarterback -- he could not very well call the next play until he saw how the last play turned out. Well, that may be a good way to run a football team, but in these days it is no way to run a government."*

Most of our leaders live in a bubble, fashioned by certain worldview and reinforced by the "yes men" who live in the bubble with him. While leaders must be deliberate and intentional if they are to be successful, turnover in team is expected and it is said to be beneficial, but excessive turnover or no turnover portends problems. Where there are changes in presidential or gubernatorial team with new appointments from time to time, it is said to contribute to a happier cabinet and, incidentally, a more disciplined one. A former United States President, Andrew Jackson said it best: *"There has been a great noise made about removals. It is rotation in office that will perpetuate our liberty."*

Right persons must be in the right positions. To all our leaders especially those with executive responsibility, I remind you of the old adage: *"It is necessary to be a fox to discover the snares and a lion to terrify the wolves."* Sometimes a leader can't always respond by brute force and must act with insight to recognise any traps. But against other opponents, like against "the wolves," a leader should be ready to show strength of a "lion" to gain respect. Creativity matters and President Buhari's team is said not to be having lots of it especially on the internal security challenges. *It was Walter Lippman that said: When all think alike, then no one is thinking."*

You may have read the Italian Renaissance thinker **Niccolò Machiavelli** most important text *The Prince* written in 1513.

In Chapter 22 of the book, Machiavelli saw that a strong prince is ultimately as good as his "servants". "The first opinion which one forms of a prince, and of his understanding, is by observing the men he has around him," wrote Machiavelli.

He says that if such "men" around the prince are "capable and faithful," then the prince will be considered wise. Otherwise, if the servants are failing, it's the prince's "error" for choosing such help.

GOING FORWARD

The word *crisis* suggests something that happens infrequently. But these days, crises have become a regular state of affairs. Removing the high percent of nepotism tendencies in our government will reduce the anxieties prevalent in the country. Nepotism is corruption and it negates the perceived integrity and love of people we associate our political leaders with.

Nigeria political leaders are very colourful in taking the needs of their followers for granted. And it is the worst behaviour in growth of electoral democracy. Hello Mr. President and all political leaders, yes, we know that every leader have constituencies. Context, as usual, explains a great deal. But balancing the complex needs of these constituencies should thus be the principal task for today's leader. You must not, escape your responsibilities to the whole country or state. And let's not get too self-righteous.

Dear friends and fellow citizens, our expectations of leadership may change with the times but, it seems, there are enduring qualifying conditions. Real leaders go first. They don't sit on the sidelines. They don't ask others to do what they are unwilling to do themselves. It is true that falling backward, especially by an older person can end up with serious injuries. Falling forward has the benefit of breaking the fall with hands and arms. We must vote falling forward.

7

Clarity of Vision |Clarity of Purpose | Clarity in Communications | Communicate to Inspire and Unite

Continuous effort – not strength or intelligence –
is the key to unlocking our potential
Winston Churchill

Precision of communication is important, more important than ever
in our era of hair trigger balances, when a false or misunderstand
word may create as much disaster as a sudden thoughtless act.
James Thurber

NIGERIANS SAID THAT THEY CAN LIVE WITHOUT certainty from a leader, but not without clarity. And there is no prophesy without talking. *Clarity* is the preoccupation of an effective and meaningful oriented *leadership*. Being clear as a leader means being simple, understandable, and exact. Leaders must also communicate as often as possible. Being a leader is not an identity, but rather, a set of actions. It's not someone you are. It's something you do. With most of our leaders, it's hard to judge the results of their agendas because there are often no real defined agendas. Nigerians are now asking that each future leader said with sufficient clarity what their agenda would be. This is the basic requirement and basics set the stage for everything. *For instance, in a short term, a simple goal for a president's speech or any other leader would always be clarity on the objective. Beyond stating the objectives, it would be good if leaders also identified the ways and means of meeting those objectives. It is also essential that the ways and means are commensurate.* A leader's main skills are her or his ability to ascertain the right thing to do (judgement) and the ability to convey ideas (clarity). A follower is influenced by a weighted average of what he or she hears. The listener places relatively greater weight on the words of relatively clearer communicators; they are better placed to coordinate him with others.

Clarity Makes Direction Unquestionable

From the perspective of Will Mancini, followers of a leader cannot travel an unmarked path. The leader's compass can't be broken; the trumpet blast can't be uncertain. There is no appreciation of uniqueness without clarity first. It was a piquant coincidence that I started the trans-creation work on the demands for speech and vision clarity by all political leaders at all levels of government in Nigeria on this day (May 10), the date on which late Winston Churchill became Prime Minister of Great Britain. The late former Prime Minister was a man known to speak with a clarity that ensured the meanings are not missed. *When he talks about the future, it is based on a clarity that is past and present.* His words to me teaches that clear vision is anchored vision. Do you not find it confusing when leaders nuance their speech instead of clearly speaking what they believe? There is absolutely no benefit for the country when presidential or gubernatorial candidates consistently over-commit, over promise, and overreach while campaigning to be elected. It is all airy promises. Let those speaking for President Buhari and the government at all levels speak always with clarity. Let leaders speak always with clarity. We want to know what the president is saying. *Aristotle called this the seat of the argument. Rhetoric fails when it does not get to the point.*

Clarity Makes Work Meaningful

Clarity really means to be free of roadblocks, obstacles... to be clear on purpose. You need to have a simple understanding of what you want and to be clear, exact in how you will reach your vision. When you are clear about what you want, you can explain your vision to others so they can understand your vision as well. Think of clarity as the fuel of vision and action. If you are not clear about the why and how you will never lift your vision off the ground. The best leaders for the today and tomorrow are ones who speak with verbal fluency to make their points crystal clear. However, the challenge is to ensure that leader's words serve as prompts for action rather than rhetorical flourishes.

Hello leader of today and tomorrow, perceptions of president's or governor's behaviour matter: They can shape a government's ability to get things done, and even the way the country or state thinks about itself. *To put it another way: Misperception is bad. It is bad for the individual soul, and it's bad for the health of a society. It breeds division and conflict.*

The explosive growth of social media is perhaps one of the most disruptive forces in society today and has become a big part of the problem of and solution to good governance and leadership. Ordinary citizens have become not just big consumer of information but now big generator of the same. We have misinformation competing effectively with actual facts and informed opinions. Information abundance, its enabling forces, and its effects have become so pernicious. Social media induce echo chambers and group-think, beliefs that are particular to one faction, rather than a commonly-shared reality. Traditional media also contributes by cherry-picking the facts to support the views its representatives and leaders wish to advance.

This is why leaders have a special duty to be clear, honest and prudent in what they do and say; otherwise, the narrative crafted around the words will lead to confusion. Where there is confusion, people are not easily led to the truth. Moreover most people are interested in political affairs only till it affects them personally otherwise most will choose comfortable status quo. *Remember as George Orwell said: "The party told you to reject the evidence of your eyes and ears. It was their final, most essential command."*

If you're in a leadership position today, now is not the time to cowardly use nuance but to courageously speak with clarity! This eliminates all confusion and leads people to the truth instead of away from it. And if you're an average citizen, make sure the leader you are following, from ministers to governors and presidency is not speaking in nuance. It's time for them to get in the game and be clear when they speak!

Nigerians said they need people who can inspire. We need people who say, *'that's the mountain that we are going to climb together and this is the reason we're going to climb it together and this is why it's never been done and this is why we're going to be successful.* True leadership is not about being popular – it's about doing the right thing in the face of massive opposition against our efforts to shape the future.

Leaders Communicate to Influence, Inspire and Achieve Results

> I am convinced, and I want you also to be convinced, that the future of this vast country must depend, in the main, on the efforts of ourselves to help ourselves. This we cannot do if we do not work together in unity. Indeed, unity today is our greatest concern, and it is the duty off everyone of us to work so that we may strengthen it...
>
> Abubakar Tafawa Balewa

The truth is, leaders rise and fall by the language they use. The ability to speak in a way that creates an emotional bridge is one of the most admired qualities of leadership. When you put the right words to a vision or a principle, it becomes axiomatic. It begins to live! The very best leaders I studied as part of this book project *wrestle with words until they are able to communicate their big ideas in a way that captures the imagination, catalyzes action, and lifts spirits.* During that brief Nigeria glorious leadership times, Prime Minster, *Late Sir Abubakar Tafewa Balewa* [ATB] has these to say: "*I am convinced, and I want you also to be convinced, that the future of this vast country must depend, in the main, on the efforts of ourselves to help ourselves...*"

Leader's language matters. Three enduring leadership qualities came through ATB speech loud and clear: *authenticity, humility and optimism.* Leaders are supposed to be purveyors of hope. Yes, words have the power to move us. They have the power to inspire us. Words unite and divide. And if not used wisely, words can bring chaos. Effective leaders have the ability to see around the corner and instill in people the hope and belief that tomorrow is better than today.

Knowledge is power in communication and leaders must never communicate without sufficient knowledge of a subject. Humility is a very attractive trait in a leader. It is the antithesis of hubris, the excessive, arrogant pride which only tends to invite controversy. *Communication competence in terms of effectiveness and appropriateness should be a firm criterion for separating leaders of ineffective government and negligible governance from those of effective government and meaningful governance.*

DO We Understand? Simplify Without Condescending

It is essential that leaders of all levels work hard to bridge the gap between the complexities of their responsibilities and the clarity followers and opponents demand. To do so, the best effective and meaningful purposive leaders simplify without condescending. This is obviously a very difficult assignment for narcissistic leaders. *Ability to communicate and communicate truthfully is one of the important leadership traits required in the Nigeria leaders of the future.* Leaders must learn to talk to the citizens, not over their heads or through them. Very important! Leaders must avoid going off-message especially to the media and international audience. Leaders and their aides must stay on message.

In his 1989 farewell address to the American people, President Ronald Reagan corrected the simplistic notion that he was simply a great communicator by saying: *"I wasn't a great communicator, but I communicated great things," gathered from "our experience, our wisdom, and our belief in principles that have guided us for two centuries."* President Reagan was aware that his political success was due, in part, to his ability to give a good speech based on two things: "to be honest" in what you are saying, and "to be in touch with [your] audience."

To capture the attention of others and facilitate behavioural change, you must influence emotion to motivate action. President Buhari was not long ago brutally criticized, and maybe rightly, for a certain portion of his speech at a side event during the *2018 Commonwealth Head of States Meeting.* Again, the President May 2018 reported statements of *"where is the electricity?"* and *"... I don't care the opinion you have about Abacha ..."* also received massive drubbing from Nigerians. Did he adhere to the needed principles of clarity, correctness and being in touch with his audience and followers in those speeches?

So many criticise the president's two speeches as overly emotional, strategically vague, and lacking in any real substance. *The president appears on that occasion to have forgotten that credibility for a communicator extends not only to what he or she said, but also how it was said.* There is even an airy joke that every problem in President Buhari's administration is a communications problem.

On the eve of his election as president, when a reporter asked Reagan what he thought other Americans saw in him, he replied: "Would you laugh if I told you that I think maybe, they see themselves and that I'm one of them." And he added: "I've never been able to detach myself or think that I, somehow, am apart from them." What a man. Leaders must be able to put past hurts behind them and never allowed wounds to fester. If a leader can't get a message across clearly and motivate others to act on it, then having a message doesn't even matter.

Going Forward

Nigerians wants their political leaders talking to them. If we are going through transitions, explain the transition to the Nigerian people. Where people get left in the dark, they are likely to conjure up nightmares and oftentimes, those nightmares are even scarier than the truth. Nigerians wants men and women as their leaders who cooled public passions, not leaders who got them all stirred up. It's essential for the present and future leaders to know how to connect to the larger public. Leadership is about solving problems. Good leaders would not seek to impose solutions; they sell them. Leaders must speak with clarity; because clarity of thought shows clarity of purpose. And yes, it can be as simple as that. Politicians worthy of our votes must be capable of combing passion with dignity and clarity with compassion.

Our people are overwhelmingly saying not again to leaders using words spectacularly: not to mobilise followers to grow the country, but to bully and belittle opponents. In the words of Nelson Mandela, 'It always seems impossible until it's done.'

8

Leaders Must Be Adaptive, Versatile, and Culturally Astute

Freedom is a fragile thing and is never more than one generation
away from extinction. It is not ours by inheritance; it must be fought
for and defended constantly by each generation, for it comes only
once to a people. Those who have known freedom and then lost it
have never known it again.
Ronald Reagan

The future is what we make of it. We owe it to ourselves to give of our
best to build the foundations of a harmonious and integrated nation,
peaceful, prosperous and vigilant, a haven of tolerance, harmony and
progress in the stormy seas of Southeast Asia.
Lee Kuan Yew

THERE IS AN ESTABLISHED NOTION that leadership is as varied as
the range of practicing leaders and the contexts in which they operate.
*But it is awful to judge a president or any leader to be cold, callous and
indifferent, especially in times of crisis. Nigerians general advice to our
leaders is to get involved, show interest, and help people out.* Building a
picture up from only narrow team or an individual is ethically wrong,
but it also demonstrates an ignorance of the nature of complex systems
such as our country and communities.

At the core of such thinking was that leaders should be *adaptive,
versatile, and culturally astute.* These concepts are fundamental for
much of the thinking of leaders required to achieve effective outcomes in
a given context. However, little attention has been given to explicitly
associating Nigeria leaders with these concepts. The two poems in the
beginning of the chapter by Ronald Reagan and Lee Kuan Yew may be
instructive in helping us to understand that there are many sources of an
effective leader's power - *awareness, astuteness, compassion,
collaboration, diplomacy, development and the power of the country's
ideals.* Leaders need to be using them all.

With the challenges the country is facing today, it's going to take an innovative approach. We need to come together to demand them. In the meantime, we need to do what we can, collectively and as individual, to fight injustice and support its victims. Remember, if you learn the adaptive skills of "follower-ship," you will have exactly the same skills you need to use when you are the leader. Being a follower is about feeling empowered and this is what this book is written to offer.

In Nigeria politics, we lionize leadership. However, how much do we really know about what makes a great leader? Worldwide, great deals of time have been spent thinking about how leadership qualities might be detected; so that leaders could be identified in advance of their elevation. For the good of the country, every attempt must be made to see that more good leaders are voted for in the next general election cycle. The time to *act is now. Just as the values of previous generations shaped history, so the values we collectively choose to live by today will shape our future.*

Incorporating Good Negotiation

There is an old saying that goes: "*You never miss your water until your well runs dry.*" Which our current leaders can we honestly say those words about when he or she leaves public service political arena? I have no hesitation as many other Nigerians in saying those about *Abubakar Tafawa Balewa, Obafemi Awolowo or Nnamdi Azikiwe.* All the three men are known for their great understanding of human interaction. They are expert in trying to answer the question of: *how might we engage with other human beings in a way that leads to better understandings and agreements?* They are known to have served, not out of arrogance, but out of a desire to make the country better for all of us, not just a few. Are we very confident saying the same thing about the current political leaders? None of the class of 2015/2018 measure up to these historical greats.

Talking about human interaction, I am beginning to have some fear and concerns about next Nigeria general elections cycle. Whatever happens at the voting booths; *however, many days it takes to know the final results of the presidential voting, half the country will feel some combination of anger, alienation, shame, sadness, despair, fear, impotence, rage, and hopelessness.* I have no doubt that many would be thinking that our country is headed in unimaginably bad direction that they have no place in this future, that the person who will be in power at the top represents everything that they are most deeply against that the system is broken that this is not who we are.

Is President Buhari culturally astute? I know or can argue at some length that Buhari's political success was/is largely based on his ability to establish deep emotional ties with a great section of the Nigerian electorate. He came with powerful appeal; the truth of which is an open subject to some, but not to his supporters. That message was and is that dark night has engulfed Nigeria or is fast approaching to totally engulf the country and a dark night from whose terrors only him at this time is specifically and particularly qualified to save us. Although it's not possible to resolve every conflict through negotiation and concession, it is feasible in most cases.

For Nigeria's Future, Parties and Leaders Must find Common Ground

Nigeria faces a long period of uncertainty, with few palatable options and most are caused by elected leaders. Effective political leadership requires the art of compromise. *As former US President Gerald Ford once said, "Compromise is the oil that makes governments go."* Why is it so difficult for Nigerian politicians to have compromising attitude and understanding? Our country is losing and losing in all fronts as a result of selfishness of our elected political leaders. *Nigerians are now saying: elect only leaders capable of taking some responsibility from the president to the local government chairmen. Our need for compromise is as great as ever. Why are leaders elected? I made series of searches and all I could see is that we elect leaders to solve problems among others. The system is proving "rigged."* Our nation's thought leaders need to develop and agree to principles now to mitigate the looming threat posed by our unstable system.

Compromise and loyalty do go hand in hand. If you want to be a good leader or follower, you must do everything you can to directly and openly engage the individuals with whom you disagree. However, loyalty demands that once a decision is made by the leader or a consensus is reached by the team, you need to practice the art of compromise and proceed with the final decision as if it were your own.

Campaigning and Governing Mindset Must be Different

To govern effectively, governing political leaders must find ways to reach agreements with their opponents, but we are not doing enough of it in Nigeria. The country is preparing for the next general election cycle, but still, the expectations raised by the previous campaign and the winner's cake sharing challenges continue to hang over the business of governing. Even when elected leaders recognise the desirability of compromise, their staunchest supporters still want to hold them to their dubious self-centeredness ideas, and believe that they exaggerate the need for concessions. Individual egos are playing a damaging role in our democratic politics.

Nigeria democratic politics will remain in crisis until we mature into situations where we have the mindset needed for governing bigger than the mindset needed for campaigning. What we have always for many years are situations where the presidency and legislative houses mindsets useful for campaigning overtakes the mindset needed for governing. As this continue to be the case, leaders--wherever they stand on the political spectrum--are less likely to see, let alone seize, opportunities for desirable compromise. The country democratic politics is making governing more difficult, by obstructing compromise, and it is bad for every one of us.

The disintegrating episode in December 2014 and July 2018 in our political parties are all results of not having compromising attitude. Nigerians are expressing an increasingly strong preference for their political leaders in Abuja and other state capitals to compromise, rather than stick to their principles at the cost of getting nothing done. With no obvious political nation building core beliefs, you will expect the politicians especially in the same political party to work together. No. This is mainly because of unnecessary categorization of bad and good boy's attitude. Too bad!

Different leaders may have different makeups, different strengths and challenges. The best leaders are focused on solutions. And good leaders accept that there are not only predetermined solutions. Followers must also understand that there are hardly predetermined solutions. Governor Akinwunmi Ambode of Lagos State has the same responsibility as my able State Governor, Willie Obiano of Anambra but the results of their actions or in-actions are basically different and are expected to be different. Again, this is as a result of the different conditions and even cultural context. In other words, good leadership is largely personality in the right place. The performances of the two governors are different because in addition to the people, the values and beliefs of influential past leaders of the two states are also different.

Good leaders adapt their thinking, formations, and governance techniques to the specific situations they face. This requires an adaptable, innovative mind, a willingness to accept prudent risk in unfamiliar or rapidly changing situations and the ability to adjust based on continuous assessment. Thriving in a rapidly changing environment depends on an innovative, responsive president, state governors, legislators and public service that excel in collaboration. Responsibilities and opportunities vary across jurisdictions. The culturally astute leader is inclusive of every person and strives for ethical decisions when planning the future. Hello Mr. President, Mr. Governor and Mr. Senator, leadership requires knowledge and experience but, most of all, it must be founded on other-centeredness, and you are not doing enough of it. Those who say compromise is a sign of weakness misunderstand the fundamental strength of our democracy.

Presidency can be More Productive with Design Thinking

Employing elements of design thinking is capable of changing the culture of failures in our presidency. The failures are even worse at the state and local government area levels. It is time for our various legislative houses to wake up. It is time to elect only people with thinking brain as legislators. Design thinking is a process of integrative thinking, a process rooted in the ability to examine and exploit opposing ideas and constraints to create solutions. Where sufficient design thinking is employed, the different departments within the presidency will be working much better together and constant failures will be reduced. In addition, the constant negative debate between the presidency and legislative house will be more amicable. People must be put at the center of our problem solving if our democratic politics and governance are to be improved. Nigeria is officially the centre of poverty and most of the politicians with power of authority to effect and affect productive and meaningful economic growth; economic transformation and improved healthcare and well-being developmental change are busy thinking on how best to win the next election.

I am strong advocate that President Buhari in his three years have shown that a four-year term is a sufficient duration for a leader to make a visible difference in the development of a country. The Bukola Saraki Presidency of the Senate has also demonstrated that much can be legislated in a single term presidency. Think about it; if the presidency has collaborated much better and productive trust established with the National Assembly, the past three years would have been much better for Nigerian people. Going forward, let us only elect people who have or can demonstrate the ability to collaborate with other people.

Going Forward

Leaders must be ready to adapt to the constant change in the local and global conditions. Think about it, when marathon runners hit start lines, they have no way of knowing what may befall them on the circuit, so adapting to race conditions is critical to finishing well. Adaptation and cultural astuteness are the keys to survival.

For now, the Nigeria political system is unworkable. The system scoffs at and ridicules the voters. The system must be changed.

Even among us reading this page and this book, I am extremely worried of us and our democratic politics participation. We all accept the need to deepen our democracy and electoral politics and yet we euphorically rationalises every dodgy election results.

We can make a start by making a decision on who we decide to follow. Let's, then, fellow-citizens, unite with one heart and one mind to ONLY vote for persons who are adaptable, flexible and cultural astute. Doing a good job is not enough; you must be culturally astute. Not every place in the Nigeria is the same. It is, therefore, imperative to identify those leaders with a strong ability to grow and adapt to fundamentally different and increasingly complex responsibilities.

9

Are You a Trusted Leader? Then Take Personal Responsibility

My boy, may you live to your full potential, ascend to as dizzy a height
as is possible for anyone of your political description in your era to
rise. May you be acknowledged world-wide as you rise
like an eagle atop trees, float among the clouds, preside
over the affairs of fellow men ... as leaders of all
countries pour into Nigeria to breath into her ear.
Nnamdi Azikiwe

When we are no longer able to change a situation, we are
challenged to change ourselves.
Viktor Frank

Don't take their apologies; they lied, they falsified, they
changed figures, they made fake promises and
they say we shouldn't talk about them.
Bola Ahmed Tinubu

MOST ARE INDECISIVE, lacking real-world experience, afraid of speaking their minds, constantly moving from blue to yellow back to blue or red, and devoid of colourful personal lives - no wonder Nigerians don't like politicians any more. We have a crisis on our democratic politics and the men and women at the wheel are principally responsible for it. The lack of quality in our political top tier is weird if you think about it – because politicians are actually very important to us. We're at a time in our history when leadership is more important than ever. However, we cannot change our political leaders until we are able to change those who elect them.

What is the way out? I take seriously the idea that we all have missions in life that we need to heed. We are responsible. Consequently, if it is required to choose one leadership lesson, one quality that stands out above all others and key to our ability to make change, create opportunity and win in this country, it would be *personal responsibility*. I wish to maintain that this sense of personality responsibility is the essential ingredient needed to resolve the tension in our democratic politics.

A certain American, Oliver North, famously stated in the year 1987, "I was authorized to do everything that I did." *No, Oliver North! Two words: personal responsibility. And we have so many Oliver North in Nigeria's political leadership class and public service leaders and managers.*

Nigeria isn't polarized about politics. It's polarized about responsibility. We need a new era of taking responsibility. Think about it. How often do you turn on the television, listen to the news, or read a magazine article, only to hear our politicians, from the presidency to legislative houses, tell you what the other guy is doing wrong and why it is not his or their fault? That if only Aishat, Yemisi, Oriaku or Jumoke would straighten up and do something, things would turn around. They promise you it is not them; they are working hard and doing all can be done to get this country back on track. Make no mistake: the "Not Me-ism" in our society is a huge problem. "They" are always at fault. *The Presidency will tell you it is the legislature especially Senate and the Senate leadership will blame the Presidency. Who is right and who is wrong.* The legislature we all should know is designed to be controversial, noisy, and sometimes even rowdy—because making laws means we have to hash out matters about which we don't all agree.

Without personal responsibility, we can never move forward, we can never build relationships and we can never hope to execute any type of plan. Harry Truman in one of his numerous remarks reminded us that every strong leader knows the "Buck Stops Here; that success and failure begin and end with you, the leader." Character requires personally demonstrating responsibility, and fairness.

Our leaders in the presidency and various state government and legislative houses must take individual responsibility and truthfully

71

allow the next election cycle to be determined by the people. After that comes governance. On that, the former Governor of Lagos State, Senator Bola Ahmed Tinubu was strong and showed personal responsibility when he said, *"Elections are not the climax of an epic book. They are merely the close of the book's opening chapter. What comes afterwards - governance is much more vital than politics, for governance determines how we shall live."*

Good governance requires leaders with big dreams and thoughts. There has been too much finger pointing in governance. Politicians demagogue the issue, but offer few real solutions. Why? Because no one wants to own the problem. It's time for that to stop. That's not leadership, and it's not responsibility. The fact is everyone owns some piece of this problem. Hello Mr. President, on the federal level, the buck stops with you. Mr. Governor, on the state level, the buck stops with you. Stand up and take the responsibility or get out! Leaders must not only have valuable visions; it must also be exposed and shared. Tinubu's description of the vision captures the ability both to see what is needed and to provoke action. Getting to a point where everyone does their part requires more than just a call to action. It will take a shift in a collective mindset that has developed because we have allowed an incredibly important personal responsibility trait to slowly leach out of our society's character.

It's Not the Circumstances, It's You!

There are dark clouds on the horizon. The country is more malleable than you think and it's waiting for you and me to hammer it into shape. It is not only what we do, but also what we do not do, for which we are accountable. Leading by example is a big responsibility, but it is not a difficult one to bear. Let's be honest; doing the right thing is usually not hard. It isn't what you are doing but how you are doing it. This is what makes all the difference. Therefore, any future leader at any level of government in Nigeria should better be prepared to do everything possible for the present and the future of the country.

I totally agree with those who said: Regardless of the situation we find ourselves in, we can choose how we respond to it. Even if we cannot change the situation itself, we can choose to change how we look at it and how we respond to it. I recently read a great quote from *Viktor Frankl, a neurologist, psychiatrist, and a Holocaust survivor that I hadn't seen before. He said, "When we are no longer able to change a situation, we are challenged to change ourselves."*

Personal Responsibility is Important

Personal responsibility has implications beyond ethics. Here are productive symbolic ideas: *Leading is courageous. To understand leadership, one must understand followership. Followership is a position with clear requirements. Followership is to choose, implicitly or explicitly, to align ourselves with another's ideas and thoughts, perhaps committing ourselves to what we believe are a greater good. Followership is a generative force that propels a country forward. Followership is closely linked to motivation — both intrinsic and extrinsic. Great leaders remove barriers to intrinsic motivation, and carefully administer extrinsic motivational inducements to nurture desired behaviours.*

What can and should our next political leaders do about it? The 2015 general election did not surprise great percentage of the population and our friends outside the country, but the 2019 will. History can teach us a great deal or as Mark Twain once said, "History doesn't repeat itself precisely, but sometimes it does rhyme." It will surprise so many because the country, I think, appears more divided and much more frustrated, much, much more frustrated and I think also angry and fearful. It's one thing to blame the powerful and the politicians for our lot, but where does personal responsibility begin and blame end in this regard. One of my favourite poetess, social entrepreneur and good governance advocate (Juliet 'Kego) once said: *"the most difficult part of achieving the TRANSFORMATION we so need as a nation, is not in changing our leaders, rather, it is in actually CONVINCING CITIZENS that they DESERVE much better. MEDIOCRITY, HYPOCRISY and DOCILITY are to me, huge blocks to societal transformation."*

Having to convince citizens in 21st century that they deserve more and can get more can only be regarded as a sign of trouble in the country development. The trouble with the trouble is that it spreads if it is not attended. I think that once there is a potential for success, we have to take it. Without the will to take risks or show boldness, we can never fulfil our vision or accomplish much of what we desire. To make sure we have the desired present and future leaders in charge of day to day activities of this great country, let's agree to take personal responsibility. Recognizing that the outcome of your life is a product of your decisions is what accepting personal responsibility is all about. It is defined as a person's 'response-ability,' that is, the ability of a person to maturely respond to the various challenges and circumstances of life.

Voters Have Responsibility and It Matters

If we want better government, we need to be better voters. With the next general election days fast approaching, it's worth asking: what is a voter responsible for doing? Terry Newell in a very important article published in *"Huffington post"* asked the same very important question and offered possible answers. Although his case study is United States, his conclusions are very suitable for voters in Nigeria as well.

According Terry Newell, voting responsibly mean at least four things. *First,* it does mean voting. All those who rail against "politics as usual" and the power of elites, big money and narrow interests can bring about change, but only if they vote.

Second, it means serious thinking. Voters need to look at candidates and issues without pre-set prejudices or the tendency to rationalize the faults of their preferred candidate. They need to subject all politicians to the requirement to prove statements through facts and defend positions by logical argument. They need to think in greater depth than headlines and sound bites. Even such supposedly thoughtful exercises as presidential debates are essentially campaign ads and boxing matches, in which a "round" is little more than three minutes, hardly enough time to provide a coherent thought and the evidence behind it. And thinking does not mean cherry-picking facts and arguments to accord with what we "feel." It means subordinating feelings to the search for objective evidence.

Third, responsible voting means suspending judgment. In the age of cable channels, talk radio, the Internet, and social media, people have a tendency to accept at face value anything they hear as soon as they hear it, especially if it agrees with their current ideas, and to pass it along without testing its veracity. Such voters make snap judgments, which easily take on the character of permanent ones.

Finally, voting responsibly means looking out for the "aggregate interests of the community." Voters can certainly question whether a candidate proposes to give them what they want, but they also must ask whether that candidate gives the nation what it needs - and personal wants and national needs can differ dramatically. It means thinking long-term. It means sacrifice.

Being personal responsible and accountable in democratic politics are doable in Nigeria. It means standing for merit- centrism, truthfulness and not faith or ethno- centrism in our leading and following. It means sacrifice, as President George Washington once said: "not ungenerously throwing upon posterity the burden which we ourselves ought to bear." Most of us have little idea about how much our feelings and behavior shape our politics and leaders. We are role model to other people and our families. Aishat Alubankudi, an economic empowerment for those in needs, healthcare and well-being and good governance social media influencer and advocate once said: *"People are losing the plot and it is double standards. I urge you to stand for the truth. We are celebrating PDPs that decamped to APC, but castigating those who left APC. What do we actually stand for??? You are confusing me more and those who have argumentative personality would judge this update negatively."*

As in the 2015 general election, a growing body of evidence has shown that our political behaviour is governed more by emotions and less by rationality. This reflects a conventional wisdom that Nigerian electorate votes irrationally and for contradictory reasons. Most people are making decisions based on momentary feeling and not on some sound understanding of how those decisions will improve or hurt their life. Our election system is mostly a sham. We need reforms. If and when that begin to happen, there would be development and progress.

Path Forward

One of my great desires is that people must be informed. Necessary information must be made available using as many media as possible. Naturally enough, most people pay less attention to collecting and digesting information about politics than we do about families, friends and careers. Moreover, we often decide quickly on our preferred candidate, and then don't change opinions; in fact, we dig our heels in deeper, even as new information and perspectives become available. It was Abubakar Tafawa Balewa that once said: *"Let us be honest with ourselves, and let us be sincere - we know what we want, and we are sure that we can get it, and get it at the right time, provided we are not delayed by selfish quarrels. At a time like this, we must all turn our minds to Almighty God and seek His guidance and assistance - by His grace, we shall succeed."*

There are huge expectations in the next general election as always and that comes with a huge responsibility. We have to tackle them with sincerity with informed knowledge. You have a responsibility to vote if you have reached the voting age and have the freedom to vote. Where you choose not to vote, you are a part of the problem and not part of the solution. When you are a leader or have responsibility, events don't cooperate. Our electoral politics and selection of candidates and election of leaders require new foundation. Practicing personal responsibility is that solid foundation. *With the various events of July 2018 in mind, there will be many of us with the knowledge of a parable about two men in the Sermon on the Mount. One built his house on a pile of sand, and it was wiped away by a storm. The other built his house on a foundation of rock, and when storms came, "It fell not." Before now, our democratic politics and election of leaders had been built on sand. Now that it had been found out, the time had come to lay a new foundation for growth and prosperity.*

However you choose to inform yourself, it will give you confidence and peace of mind that, when you go to cast your vote, you will not be voting out of thoughtless name-recognition, or party-affiliation. This could trick you into voting against your own world-view. By taking your civic duty seriously, you not only will cast a vote, but cast an informed vote.

Going forward, President Buhari is the president today and working to come back after the next general election. I hope he does. If Nigerians voted no, it doesn't matter. Nigeria and her continual progress is what matters. As the founding fathers of the country did in 1950s and 1960s, the president has seen it all and history will judge him kindly to adhering to the values that are timeless: *duty and integrity, moral courage and sacrifice, honesty and personal responsibility.* Every generation, every age brings with it new challenges — but with good leadership and a cross-party approach, Nigeria's leaders can solve problems, get things done, improve the lives of our citizenry and lay a foundation for our children's future.

10

Leadership Requires Relationship: No Lasting Success Without It

African leaders must stand up, stand together, support one
another, and begin making decisions that please us first before
pleasing the international community.
Osasu Igbinedion

My parents; bless their souls; were both teachers but the most
important lesson that they taught our household was to love
and serve God. My faith cannot be compromised by my
political ambition; the Bible is littered with examples
of great leaders who fell by the wayside through
disobedience. Let him who has ears...
Ifeanyi Ubah

I AM GOING TO START THIS CHAPTER by stating directly that leadership begins with the long view — getting along with others, even those who oppose your views, and maintaining respectful relationships. Today's opponents might, on another issue another day, be allies. Nigeria federal government is created to be a government of laws and not of men; however, the last few years have been very tough. We are having a situation where the old saying that *"No man can be president for long without becoming, the Butt of party malevolence,"* as nicely said by as John Adams. This was the case with President Goodluck Jonathan and now for Muhammadu Buhari. Another dictum of former US President John Adams, that both President Jonathan and Buhari can be said to have associated their presidency with are that: *"gratitude, friendship, unsuspecting confidence, and all the most amiable passions in human nature,"* are the most dangerous guides in politics. Sometimes, there is the feeling that for both men, their parties wanted gnawing away; both acknowledge that everything comes to you at the right moment. In the end, we can conclude that character is destiny.

There is a way out. The challenge for Mr. President and other leaders is not just about overcoming misgivings; the ability to build bridges and relationships may be the difference between success and failure. He or she must make the rivals want to join his or her team to work for the success of the country and communities. Former US President Roosevelt was described to be "like an electric light that lit up everything around him." You can't lead unless you understand how to work with people - especially people who are different from you. That sounds obvious, but building the skills to effectively collaborate with people who are different from us - those who have unfamiliar identities, experiences, and ideas require deliberation and practice. Most of us are more comfortable working with people who think and act like we do, because they won't challenge our beliefs. Nigeria myth trumps fact to an even greater extent than elsewhere.

Going forward, Nigerians are asking for strong combinations of stubbornness and flexibility in our today and tomorrow's leaders. Both are essential for good governance. It is said that President Lincoln's success came from his empathy and ability to appreciate the position of his former rivals.

This let him connect with them and attract them to follow him. This book encourages our politicians of 2019 and beyond class to emulate President Lincoln and Prime Minister Abukabar Tafawa Balewa attitudes in their politicking and authority. Lincoln was able to keep subordinate his personal feelings and uncertainties to advance his social ambitions. In him and many others like him, I learn that capable leaders advance without coveting fame and retreat without fearing disgrace. His only purpose is to protect his people and promote the best interests of his nation and not his south or north.

The main challenge facing President Buhari today is the need to mobilize the nation to greatness. You have to do it. You don't have to poring over the writings of so-called APCs or PDPs people. It is instinctual. Those coming after you MUST come better prepared. All politics are not just local, all

" ... I am convinced, and I want you also to be convinced, that the future of this vast country must depend, in the main, on the efforts of ourselves to help ourselves. This we cannot do if we do not work together in unity. Indeed, unity today is our greatest concern, and it is the duty off everyone of us to work so that we may strengthen it. This morning I said in the House of Representatives that bitterness due to political differences would carry Nigeria nowhere, and I appealed to the political leaders throughout the country to control their party extremists. To you who are listening tonight I repeat that appeal - Let us put away bitterness and go forward in friendship to Independence ..."

Abubakar Tafawa Balewa

"And if we cannot end now our differences, at least we can help make the world safe for diversity. For, in the final analysis, our most basic common link is that we all inhabit this small planet. We all breathe the same air. We all cherish our children's future. And we are all mortal."

John F. Kennedy

Confusion reigns in the country political arena and it is slowing the country down. We need leaders to make Nigeria great. Leadership is a community and leading through relationships epitomizes effective leadership. Scholars believe that it is frequency of contact and type of contact that promotes followers to remain actively engaged with leaders. It just happens that transformational leaders do this more and better than other types of leaders. Nigerians are asking and looking for transformational leaders ONLY! Nigerians want an activist government and transformational leaders are the right mix.

Path Forward

What Nigerians said they want are effective leaders at all levels of government. Hello people, if you want the reward, you have to keep pushing forward, through every obstacle, past every peak. You can never, ever give up. Sometimes the choices are hard; so hard that we avoid making them. But inevitably, the choice will get made. If not by you, then for you. And that's never good. If we want the best outcome, we have got to stay focused on the goals, set aside our emotions and make the tough choices.

President Buhari's election and inauguration in 2015 quickly elevated Nigeria's image abroad; however, arose and endured were a blatant deterioration of relations internally in the country. Given the schoolyard mudslinging that goes for national governance, value of our lives in Nigeria has probably gone down since 2015. Just a thought. Time has come for our leaders to shift to a fairness mindset and show more empathy. You cannot effectively lead someone you don't understand.

Going forward, Nigerians are saying: *forget 'strong and stable perception' – political leadership required in Nigeria at the present stage of our development is about knowing your weaknesses. The "I alone can fix it," is the main shortcomings of the current federal government administration. No lone individual is going to be good at all. Nigeria is a diverse country and to be an effective president, you must have or acquire relating capacity. Relating-the capacity for building relationships and networks of support.*

Leaders who are strong in this area can put forward their own point of view but also ask for and listen carefully to differing opinions. You may have problems "relating" if you tend to constantly blame others for failed projects or feel they can't be trusted. It is important that Nigerians remember that the country is bigger than any one person, with values and institutions that should grow and sustain the democracy from presidency to presidency.

These are challenges and only leaders including followers can fix it. Nigerians said that self-awareness and coach-ability in leaders are at the top of the list of the qualities they are looking for in the oncoming leaders. It makes perfect sense. Today's environment requires us to adapt quickly and relentlessly. That means leaders must not only be great at what they do, they must also "know what they don't know" and be willing to work hard to learn it. *John Maxwell once wrote: "A leader is one who knows the way, goes the way, and shows the way."*

11

Emotional Courage and Intelligence Are Key To Being a Great Leader

Restructuring Is a Necessity, Not an Option. The restructured Nigeria
... is a Nigeria that not only provides opportunities for everyone to
work but even more specifically challenges every layer of governance
to demonstrate the capacity to create wealth and jobs for the citizens.
Atiku Abubakar

What makes leadership hard isn't the theoretical, it's the practical. It's
not about knowing what to say or do. It's about whether
you're willing to experience the discomfort, risk,
and uncertainty of saying or doing it.
Peter Bregman

NIGERIA IS PROBABLY IN HER WORST turbulent times; and when a country is as desperate as Nigeria is now, inspirations matters. Not just the citizens, Nigeria need inspiration. Inspiration awakens us to new possibilities by allowing us to transcend our ordinary experiences and limitations. Inspiration propels a person from apathy to possibility, and transforms the way we perceive our own capabilities. Inspiration increases well-being. Where are our country leaders? Our president and most of our other political leaders are in hiding. The inspirations we and the world welcomed and envisaged with the 2015 election results has not enabled creativity. There is a reported shortage in the required knowledge. As Rudyard Kipling once explained, *"When your Daemon is in charge, do not try to think consciously. Drift, wait, and obey."* Without complete knowledge and information, leaders' good intentions can cause significant unintended consequences. A thousand years ago, an Islamic cleric was quoted saying *"knowledge is power and it can command obedience."* Most of our political leaders are clearly not prepared or lack the needed work mastery.

Thus, challenges facing us as a country and as a people are many and daunting, enough to put fear into any rational person. As recent research shows, inspiration can be activated, captured, and manipulated, and it has a major effect on important life outcomes. But it requires emotional courage and self-awareness.

Courage is a quality obviously demanded by our time. Positions of leadership and responsibility bring with them trials, pressures, and temptations; and the greater the responsibility, the greater the temptations. Abraham Lincoln once said, "Nearly all men can stand adversity, but if you want to test a man's character, give him power." Those who lead require strong character in order to fulfil their responsibilities without losing their balance. According to David Foster Wallace, the American writer, *"Real leaders are individuals who help us overcome the limitations of our own weakness, and selfishness, and laziness, and fears, and get us to do harder, better things than we can get ourselves to do on our own."*

Something is not right in Nigeria. In Nigeria of today, President Muhammadu Buhari is the topmost leader of the Federal Republic of Nigeria. Senator Abubakar Bukola Saraki is the Nigeria Senate President and Rt. Hon. Yakubu Dogara is the honorable speaker of the House of Representatives and all the 36 Governors of the 36 States in the Federation are all topmost leaders. *We must start to get real in this country. With reference to the individuals mentioned above, most are asking Nigerians again for their support and votes in the next general election. That some of them have the boldness to seek for reelection or seek for election into another elective post, is an indication of where we are as a country.* What can we say about their qualifications? Who and who among them have really helped the country to overcome the limitations of our own weakness, and selfishness, and laziness, and fears. Do you think any of them or others not listed here have actually increased our fears and our selfishness?

All pretenses will be exposed at some point. It was Edward Murrow that once said: *"To be persuasive we must be believable; to be believable we must be credible; to be credible we must be truthful."* Leaders must make themselves and actions believable. The clearer your picture, the easier it will be for you to share it with others. Our famous Maya Angelou said, *"When someone shows you who they are the first time, believe them."* I know one or two in the list and I didn't believe them before, I believed them NOW.

Facing Fear and Failure. A little Forbearance Serves You Well

I would like to reiterate the difficulties I had writing this book. In my journey of life, an important lesson I have picked along the way is, when you're really, really scared, take one step into the fear. Move into the fear, not away from it. Don't duck it. Don't pull out and try to scroll it away. Move into it in a real time. The fear was pervasive, intellectually and morally. I had the nagging question – maybe I won't be able to accomplish ...but I did. I only did because somehow I found the courage to keep gathering all that I require to make a success of it. *I also comforted myself constantly with the wise words of Martin Buber, the 20th century German philosopher, who once said: A might purpose is always about the movement from I to thou, from me and my agenda to something bigger and more transcendent that's about other people. I have since learned that getting lost can be the best teacher. It can help you find your way!*

President Muhammad Buhari does not like to convince people and doesn't pretend about it. *Has he been a good president? Effective presidents are said to play a role unlocking others, challenging the status quo and enabling creativity and above all, uses strategic vision to motivate and inspire.* And smugness is not the way to go. He has put up with some of the nasty criticism with poise and dignity, even humor. That kind of character is admirable and rare. But I totally disagree with his approach on the nuisance of herdsmen and farmlands and his stone silence on the reported nepotism in his administration. Is he perfect? Obviously not. How could he be? Why would anyone think he might be? No one has ever. In manner and method, he is unlike his predecessors. He had so many obstacles to overcome. But situations change and new opportunities sometimes emerge. What is not possible to achieve yesterday may be possible to achieve today or tomorrow – and you have to be prepared to take advantage of the opening.

Some have argued, rightly in my view that leadership boils down to few special words: emotional courage, self-awareness, coach-ability and choice. Leaders and follower's courage, awareness and choices build upon each other and form a virtuous cycle, one feeding another.

As a candidate, President Buhari seemed keenly aware that he didn't want to repeat the mistakes of previous PDP administrations. But of course, these were other people's mistakes, not his. And now he has made different ones, and I guess some of the same ones. The president's reported refusal to change perceived non-communicating cabinet members strike directly at some of his own shortcomings. The President Buhari I know had a strong capacity for self-reflection and awareness, and for arriving at fresh solutions. That capacity is now open to question. He'd better rediscover it quickly or his presidency will have a mixed history.

You can't led without Emotional Courage

Emotional courage is one of the key strengths that effective leaders must have and it is developable. To grow and develop as humans, we need to be able to take some small (or large) steps out of our comfort zone. Not stepping out of our comfort zone breeds mediocrity and allows us to "stay safe," which in turn can keep us in a rut. Emotional courage is widely taken as the sine qua non of leadership. Without it, a person won't make a great leader in this increasingly connected, competitive, volatile, uncertain, ambiguous world. This is the courage to speak up when others are not and remaining steadfast, grounded and measured in the face of uncertainty. It means responding productively to political opposition. *Love or hate him, Nasir El-Rufai, the current executive governor of Kaduna State is an example of a leader who has increased their effectiveness in the face of uncertainty and ambiguity. His performance even as the FCT minister shows a man with confidence in critical leadership moments. His previous and current actions and reactions exemplifies how a strategic leader adjusts strategy and execution amid complex social, political, developmental and economic forces without compromising deeply held values. These are developable traits.*

Emotional courage is not a talent that some people are born with and others aren't. We all can develop it. Courage implies detailed knowledge of variables and options. It presupposes hard work and calculation as well as a sense of principles and priorities. It is a kind of wisdom. It is not compatible with mindlessly disorienting friends or strengthening adversaries. As a leader, to hold on to a view even against consensus when you are convinced of its validity is to experience social isolation for your belief in truth; this is an excellent act of emotional courage. But to relinquish false claims to knowledge in the light of more compelling evidence is no less courageous. Every time you take a risk, make a truthful decision, or influence others, you are growing your emotional courage. According to Peter Bregman, to be confident, connected and committed, simultaneously, requires tremendous emotional courage.

We have People with Emotional Courage of Ignorance as Leaders

Nigerians do not want chameleon or those with courage of their ignorance either as the president, vice president, governor, senate president, house speaker, legislator, minister, commissioner, and other political leader. Many of current class fit the dictionary.com definition of demagogue: "a person, especially an orator or political leader, who gains power and popularity by arousing the emotions, passions, and prejudices of the people."

We can say that many of our political leaders in this current 2015/2019 class have and are tapping into the deep anger in the public who hate all of our political capitals and its dysfunction. This is not new. Yes as a political leader, your followers may adore you and believe your promises and praises you because you pretend you always speak your mind. But even speaking one's mind does not mean one speaks the truth or has courage. While some instances of courage demand physical valor, every form of courage presupposes intellectual capacities. Famous Plato said courage is an intellectual virtue. With the *classic 1957 film, "A Face in the Crowd," written by Budd Schulberg in mind,* I challenge our political leaders to prove that what they have are not "courage of ignorance."

As Rhodes, the main culprit with a courage of his ignorance did in the "A Face in the Crowd," this is probably what most of the Nigeria political leaders think of the voters and followers in their closet: *"Those morons out there? Shucks, I could take chicken fertilizer and sell it to them as caviar. I could make them eat dog food and think it was steak. ... You know what the public's like? A cage of guinea pigs. Good night, you stupid idiots. Good night, you miserable slobs. They're a lot of trained seals. I toss them a dead fish and they will flap their flippers."*

Our political leaders including our presidents, governors and senators are obviously getting what they want; they are not serving the people. And it has to stop. Most of them do not have the emotional courage required for their position of responsibility. This can only continue if the informed failed in our duties to keep educating the uninformed among the people. We live in a country where it is far easier to avoid our feelings than it is to feel them. We need emotional courage to engage with our colleagues where they live, where the desire for affirmation and the fear of failure are constantly in play. Followers and leaders who cultivate emotional courage and self-awareness will thrive.

I call upon our president, governors and other political leaders to emulate Nelson Mandela by finding ways to practice forgiving without forgetting and sharing power. In one of numerous and inspiring speeches, he said: *"We have to surprise [the white minority] with restraints and generosity."* Mandela understood rallying the country and bridging diverse interests meant making room for others. Mr. President. Mr. Governor. Mr. Senator. Rt. Hon. Speaker. Mandela, after being elected South Africa's first black president, announced he would serve only one term, though two were permissible and he could easily have stayed and be reelected. I call upon our leaders to be Nelson Mandela of Nigeria! Be him in your speeches and actions. He exercised a full range of cognitive, emotional and behavioral abilities to bring about profound change in South Africa. It took a great understanding of greatness of emotional courage, self-awareness, emotional intelligence and coach-ability for Mandela to achieve all he did and how he did it. Don't insist on winning battle, but losing the war! History mostly records the wars not the battles. Wars are ever-more complex and ambiguous.

So...How Self-Aware Effective Are You?

Self-awareness to most people mean knowing what you are good at and what you are not. You don't pretend to know it all. It means you practice humility and embrace learning. Self-awareness leads to greater clarity about what we want. It is the understanding that by knowing what we want, we can create a plan to get there. A crucial part of becoming a more self-aware leader is to understand what your strengths and weaknesses are, and the best way to find this out is by gathering feedback from stakeholders. Tasha Eurich in her best-selling book *(INSIGHT: Why We're Not as Self-Aware as We Think, and How Seeing Ourselves Clearly Helps Us Succeed at Work and in Life)* said: self-awareness comprises a clarity of self, knowing who you are, understanding your behaviour patterns and passions; and finally knowing your impact on others. Eurich argues that: *"There is strong scientific evidence that people who know themselves and how others see them are happier. They make smarter decisions. They have better personal and professional relationships. They raise more mature children...They're more effective leaders with more enthusiastic employees. They even lead more profitable companies."*

We seem to get less self-aware as we get older. "Experienced leaders are more likely to overestimate their abilities," writes Eurich, "Similarly, older managers tend to misjudge their performance relative to their boss's ratings of them far more than their younger peers do." *Go ahead and ask: is Mr. President self-aware effective? How about your state governor, senator or your legislator? How about other political leaders including federal ministers? These are all legitimate questions to have.* How many times have our presidents, governors, senators, ministers and other leaders made promises that were not "fully informed" at the time? With the country in tempestuous times with a record number of unemployment, high rate of nepotism in the government, lawlessness in the society, reported daily killings by herdsmen and cattle hustlers, and preparation towards the next general election cycle, the two main political parties in the country in a failure of self-awareness picks a fight over trust and nomenclature. And the so-called lazy youth and near irrelevant adults mixed with paid agents are busy with 'APCs' is better than your 'PDPs' unproductive songs and name-calling.

Emotional Intelligence Has Dark Side

Remember the question in Chapter 1. Are you starting to wonder where all the outstanding leaders are in the country? And why it's so hard to find them at least in public office? If true leadership entails emotional intelligence—the ability to recognise, understand, and manage emotions and I believe it does — we can look to the current president and senate president as an embodiment of what truly emotionally intelligent leadership looks like.

The senate president public persona is one of strength and confidence and so is President Buhari. The President of the Nigeria Senate, Abubakar Bukola Saraki, shows empathy when things go wrong; he shows heart and humor when things go right. It's not easy. It takes practice. We all mess up from time to time. But it's good to have a leader or leaders who at least seem to understand what emotional and social intelligence is, who can model what skillful behaviour looks like. You may think that's just all part of being a politician? Compare Bukola Saraki to Ken Nnamani. Or Buhari to Obasanjo to Goodluck Jonathan, one of those can be judged to be politically smart and personally charming, but had some issues with impulse control. One of the things you sense about Saraki and leaders like him is this deep well of self-confidence. And that's really important … And I think on top of that he has this spacious intellect. I mean he has not only read a lot, but he's absorbed it.

President Buhari has a very high-level of emotional intelligence. He definitely devoted his talent with unrelenting focus to achieving his dreams. I have no doubt that President Buhari taps into the deep emotional needs of many people in the country. Most of us are feeling defeated and powerless to stop the debilitating corruption in the country, the infrastructural decay all over the country and airy promises in Abuja, and the ever-growing economic divide. That shows in him an understanding of emotions and the ability to put that understanding to use. That understanding and ability to use it makes up part of emotional intelligence.

Emotional intelligence is the accepted catalogue of competencies such as real humility, transparency, integrity, accountability, empathy among other elements for managing needed good governance in Nigeria. *A valid question to ask: is the government of President Buhari emotionally intelligent? Feel free to ask of that for any of the state government and local government areas.*

Just like an individual, a government needs to be emotionally intelligent in order to first understand, manage and direct itself effectively, to then be able to understand, manage and direct its people.

Emotional intelligence is not an only positive trait. President Buhari, President Jonathan, Vice President Atiku or even the current Senate President, Bukola Saraki could all be emotional intelligent but each of them could also be sociopath. Sociopaths with a high-level of emotional intelligence, have the ability to disguise their true feelings and use their understanding of others for their own personal gain. Going forward, it is legitimate to ask and know between the leadership candidates who are only using the emotions of the people for personal gain. There is no doubt that many of our political leaders have been wrongly using emotions to deceive majority of our uninformed citizens. We must reject such people and deny them occupation of public office. So much misperceptions in our society.

Ability to be Coachable, Nigerians Said is Must

Valuable leaders must be coach-able. Who among the contending leadership candidates are open to feedback and are willing to take action to change behaviour. *Leaders who are not coachable can have such symptoms as: inflated self-importance, ego gone awry, inability to work with different types of people, overuse of position power, poor use of communication and influence skills, inability to form functioning teams, and inability to change.* Political party leaders must not select or allow people who lack such capacity to represent them. Voters must reject future leaders with any of the attributes.

Going Forward

Nigeria is most divided about political opinion than it ever was before. It is important when striving to live a good life that we are aware of our ability to choose and exercise our choice rather than settle for the default option. The default setting is usually designed to cater to our need for convenience or laziness. Being aware of choice is also synonymous with being conscious. Next time any leadership position candidate talks to you about voting for him, make sure the person is able or willing to separate truth from falsehood. She or he does encourage conflicting views. He doesn't lack self-control or acts impetuously. He can tolerate criticism and understand the principles of separation of powers. Make sure that the future leader asking for your support has the ability to facilitate good conversation and tell the truth.

It was Mark Zuckerberg of FACEBOOK that once said, "It is not enough to have purpose yourself. You have to create a sense of purpose for others." Let's hope that Nigeria will see as many great leaders as ones who practice democratic conversationalism in any arguments and discussions so that other people are invited into various circumstances.

12

Beware of Candidate with Narcissism and Comprehension Deficient Syndrome

Democracy cannot succeed unless those who express their choice are
prepared to choose wisely. The real safeguard
of democracy, therefore, is education.
F.D. Roosevelt

The true nature and intention ... of a writer's work does
not lie within his own knowledge.
Rudyard Kipling

SOMETIMES WINNERS ARE CONVERTED to losers in our country. The above quote of Roosevelt is another reminder why this book is written. Nigeria is an interconnected chaos of reality and it is very difficult to make sense just by looking at it. Just look at all the cognitive sick and serial pretenders we have in our political leadership. In the broader political economy literature, the conventional wisdom suggests that voter ignorance is a prime factor for why criminal or corrupt politicians win elections. In some ways, when people feel powerful or feel powerless, it influences their perception of others.

There's old saying: power corrupts. Dishonesty and power go hand-in-hand. Columbia Business School findings suggest people in power make better liars. Does political power in Nigeria attract dishonest people or does political power in Nigeria make people dishonest? Reading a study of Joe Magee, a researcher and professor of management at New York University, you will learn that power isn't corrupting; it's freeing. What power does is that it liberates the true self to emerge. Once you get into a position of power, then you can be whoever you are, he says. We have had at least in the last ten years proof that the Nigeria has entered an era of what David Roberts called "post-truth" politics: a political culture in which debate is framed largely by appeals to emotion disconnected from the details of policy, and by the repeated assertion of talking points to which factual rebuttals are ignored or what Stephen Colbert, an American comedian, calls "truthiness": *ideas which feel right or should be true.* Some have argued that dishonesty in politics is nothing new; but the manners in which some politicians now lie, and the havoc they may wreak by doing so, are worrying. In 1986 President Ronald Reagan insisted that his administration did not trade weapons for hostages with Iran, before having to admit a few months later that: "My heart and my best intentions still tell me that's true, but the facts and evidence tell me it is not." *I make bold to ask our president and governors, are there things you need to admit?* Nigeria politicians are getting away with a new depth and pervasiveness of falsehood and it is dangerous to allow the practice to continue. The power of the leader is dependent on the gullibility of the followers. The greatest threat to our democracy is our own willingness to tolerate dishonesty in pursuit of power.

You probably know someone who gained political or economic power and suddenly manifest a near damaging self-centred values and selfishness that you never know he or she has. Are the leaders you are supporting or working for self-aware? Is he or she coach-able? If they are, perhaps, they will realize the dangers inherent in practice of power if used wrongly and correct themselves. Otherwise, they are deliberately narcissistic, serial pretender and fibbing prone, and we should keep such people away from gaining political leadership responsibility.

Nigeria situation has been made worse by a chorus of enablers who defend every lie of lying politicians. According to the Former New York City Mayor Michael Bloomberg, when we tolerate dishonesty, we get criminality. Sometimes, it's in the form of corruption. Sometimes, it's abuse of power. And sometimes, it's both. Politicians can just say anything to create realities. Most times our people do not really know who among the politicians are for them because people are impoverished and almost deliberately kept uneducated. You can say that the former US President Roosevelt took aim at what Nigeria is facing so many years ago; asserting that democracy cannot succeed unless those who express their choice are prepared to choose wisely. The real safeguard of democracy, therefore, is education.

The Truth is Out There

The materials for this chapter were very difficult to transcreate and conclusions drawn sufficiently. In the end, I concluded it needs to be done. I hope you will find the interpretations enlightening as I did. Why must it pay to be outrageous, but not to be truthful in Nigeria of today? As a leader or follower, accountability is one of the attributes we get many opportunities to practice. We are constantly confronted with decisions and choices that test us. I wouldn't have practiced what I have preached in the previous chapters if I am to omit this chapter. The truth is out there. Let's find them. It will not be pain-free. To keep going, I found solace in the portion of *Rudyard Kipling (IF poem published in a collection of short stories entitled Rewards and Fairies):*

> If you can force your heart and nerve and sinew
> To serve your turn long after they are gone,
> And so hold on when there is nothing in you
> Except the Will which says to them: "Hold on!"
> …
> If you can talk with crowds and keep your virtue,
> Or walk with kings – nor lose the common touch

Kipling's writing has inspired many to find meaning in his words that may be well beyond what Kipling intended and I am one of the many. Kipling believed that a reader should find the truth in a writer's words. He once said, "The true nature and intention … of a writer's work does not lie within his own knowledge." Success in life is all about focus. Each person has something exceptionally to offer the world. And reality is what truth is about. Voting for a political candidate is leading. Once we decide to lead, we must learn to lead well. The more we learn, the more choices we see, and the cycle continues.

Hello Nigerians, it is essential that we know what we have and where we are going to. We know that without abstraction and generalisation, there can be no thought-I couldn't have written this book. We also know that accuracy of data is the pre-condition of any historical work. But in the end, what determines the quality of a historian is the quality of his judgement. And this chapter and the next are historical. Fear is one emotion that has predominantly marked the social and psychological landscape of middle and upper middle-class Nigeria over the past decade. Fear of speaking up and speaking out, fear of running afoul of the powers that be and consequences, fear of continual unemployment, fear of continuous nepotism in government, fear of continual debilitating corruption, fear of daily criminal activities and killings around the country. Yes, the last general election was highly polarized, both along class and racial/ethnic lines. If you take the two ingredients—dysfunctional government and deep social cleavages—they go a long way to explaining the popularity of the strongman rule. I have seen no reason to feel anything different in the next election. The current federal government administration appears to be talking and listening. However, not all talking is thinking. Nor does all listening foster transformation.

But there is but...

There is so much insecurity and false communication and insufficient care for the other person. The historical killing of so many Nigerians especially in areas around Jos today ... is on my mind this hour. History will not forgive many of us for shying away from the truth because of our cowardly attitude of defending what is indefensible. *It was George Bernard Shaw that famously warned that we should "beware of false knowledge; it is more dangerous than ignorance."*

There is Anger in the Air

There is anger and at the same time intolerance around the country, and rightly so. Many Nigerians are mad as hell at our political leaders. We live in a moment when our collective faith in government, business, and religion is waning. One can easily observe various forms of anger that are shaping the public discourse in Nigeria, and the public sphere and civil society. There's no question we have a leadership vacuum. It's not confined to the executive but also with legislative arms of government, judiciary and across the political spectrum. I thought Dele Momodu is correct when he said: "The level of despicable intolerance I see is unprecedented in my 58 years on earth. I shudder to think what will happens if these enraged youth spill over their vitriol & venon from the fantasy & imaginary world of the cloud into the real & visible world of the streets."

The anger is understandable. The anger derives equally from governmental ineptitude, arrogance and corruption, and self-serving politicians more concerned with getting re-elected than with the country's future. This void is partly a result of the lapses of integrity and judgment and decency that contributed to the political and economic crisis of the past 50 years - and regrettably, many of these lapses were never made right, just as many of the people responsible for them were not really held accountable.

Governance outcomes are products of deliberate actions, in-actions and reactions. I ask you; are the current and previous president(s) and vice president(s) corrupt? Is the Senate president corrupt? Are the state governors corrupt? What do we think of their close associates? No, they are not. But, none is immune to that possibility. Yes, every one of them has very high integrity! If they are what they claim they are; it is troubling to have our country still operating at the level we are. Pick any of the presidents and you will find that the media and their supporters would have contrasted the president's supposed honesty and forthrightness with other president's supposed venality and political unscrupulousness. Human responsibility ultimately requires not only simple vision and rudimentary intelligence, but also some basic honesty. Wherever there is one without the other, there can be no decent human society. It's not complicated. We must encourage our politicians to be honest in their dishonesty and live the truth. Always, truth is exculpatory.

Is All this Rage Pervading the Country Genuine and Righteous?

Anger counteracts apathy. Many people feel that they have been wronged, and they are compelled to fight. But it can also go too far. Anger doesn't just activate the go system; it drops a heavy brick on the gas pedal. It is a force that motivates people to speak up and act, but it can also make them less effective in doing so. After studying activists, Debra Meyerson and Maureen Scully suggest that the key is to be "simultaneously hot and cool-headed. The heat fuels action and change; the coolness shapes the action and change into legitimate and viable forms." Nigerians are generally known for having a positive outlook on life, but with the countdown to 2019 presidential election now well under way; polls show voters are both hot- and cool-headed. We are all that way and that's a problem. I am believer that anger is alluring in the short-run, but ultimately happiness-eroding. It's quick, it's binary, and it's delicious. Anger is an empowering emotion: we don't feel weak or low when we are angry; rather we feel strong and dominant. Anger is triggered by thoughts related to fairness: we feel angry when we think that others have treated us unfairly. And more and more Nigerians are gorging on it. Our political leaders have surely treated the citizens unfairly. The catch is that rage uncorked becomes rage indulged, and rage indulged becomes rage applauded.

In deciding about this book and reading through thousands of comments sent in by Nigerians on the subject of excellent leadership, I became angry. In trans-creating and understanding the rich comments, I am angry. Psychologically speaking, the important thing is not the emotion, but what we do with it; whether we vent, process or suppress it. Positively, anger provokes us to change an unjust situation, and in this case, I made this rewarding decision to write this book (which is really a letter to my country men and women). *"If I wish to compose or write or pray or preach well, I must be angry, Martin Luther King once said. Then, all the blood in my veins is stirred, and my understanding is sharpened."* Unprocessed anger pollutes the social sphere. Most broad, collaborative calls for change begin with a story that enrages people. It is on that reasoning that this book is written.

After the September 11th, 2001, attacks, TIME's Lance Morrow wrote a powerful essay titled, *The Case for Rage and Retribution, in which he argued: "For once let's have no fatuous rhetoric about 'healing.' A day cannot live in infamy without the nourishment of rage. Let's have rage. What's needed is a unified, unifying, Pearl Harbor sort of purple American fury - a ruthless indignation that doesn't leak away in a week or two..."* If Martin Luther King and Lance Morrow views are true, then, Nigerians will have to be angrier than we are presently for the country to move forward. What our politicians including our beloved president doesn't understand is that you can't be a prophet to the culture while you're standing outside of the room. We all must rise up and ask every one of the politicians: "What are they doing? Not, what are they saying? Examples are available of leaders who have through their actions and in-actions incited animosity and indeed hatred among certain groups of their citizens toward their fellow citizens. Such emotions are negative and never beneficial. According to Nancy Koehn, leaders who have risen to power by relying heavily on collective anger and discrimination toward other groups have proven to be despots, tyrants, and men who destroy the values and institutions that lie at the heart of democracies. Such people are part of our democratic politics and Nigerians should better reject.

Comprehension Deficient | Narcissism is Good Only When It Behaves

Effective governance in Nigeria is still struggling to put down deep roots maybe we are too impatient for change, and too intolerant of views that are different from ours. That we know. We also know that Nigerians said they need leaders who can see the nuance in situations, who don't collapse the country into simple *North West, North East, North Central, South East, South South and South West categories. We need leaders who sees people as people and not 'he is a Christian or 'he is a Muslim.'*

Some of our political leaders and their associates are doing that. Cognitive distortion is not a great habit in a leader. In the course of the research for this book, I have read most of texts in the public domain about all of our past presidents and present president. I have also followed the activities of some of the state governors and the legislators. I have been watching all the presidential candidates for the 2019 general election with great interest and deep concern. Concern for people I admire and love who find themselves midst of Nigeria power play and are drained of most of their goodness. I am concerned on the fate of our country in general. I have no privileged information; like any other intellectual, I read the newspapers, follow the news, and discuss current affairs with friends and colleagues. Paraphrasing President Kagame, I say to you: *"Don't allow yourself to be put down by negative things around you. Keep showing up and saying I can do something for myself and for the country."*

Yes, we can and we have the power to shape the future of this great country. However, beware of depraved cabals prominent at all levels of our government! These depraved cabals operating with so much responsibility with no accountability has a stranglehold on Nigerian political and financial power. It didn't start with the present administration and will probably not end with them. They have always constituted type of totalitarianism pillaging the country through barbaric annihilation.

Fellow Nigerians, to allow yourself to think of these people as foolish, incompetent, irrational, or wrong-headed is as mistaken and misinformed as thinking that Hitler was merely a well-meaning but mistaken fearless leader of his people.

To all adults in the house, we must beware at an occasion like this of what's been called *narcissistic personality syndrome, comprehension deficient syndrome with a dab of delusions of grandeur.* Narcissism is not a diagnosis. Comprehension deficient is not a diagnosis. They have never been.

Narcissists are people higher in narcissistic traits than the average person, and while they may or may not be disordered, they all share one thing in common: they feel special. These people have an inflated sense of their own importance, a deep need for excessive attention and admiration, and a lack of empathy for others. Narcissists have difficulty forging long-term relationships. Because narcissists are continuously seeking recognition from others to reinforce their own self-worth, they tend to form new relationships where they can see a positive reflection of themselves in the other person's eye. Think about it – look at what is happening at our two main political parties – PDPs and APCs. Narcissist politicians are happy to stand side by side with undefined elements for re-election gains. Must you carry on winning and leading longer than you have? Is it not a special privilege to lead a nation or state or Senate for a year? These guys have the belief that everything in the country is about them. To people with such understanding, it is either we did or said something, or didn't do or didn't say something, or if we did something or said something, it would all be well. Narcissists are always preoccupied with power, prestige, vanity, and thinks they deserve special treatment and fame. Does anyone want to prove that most of our present political leaders are not? Don't waste your time proving – most are. We should rather be more concerned about how healthy they are. And that's where you come in.

Let's avoid narcissistic leaders – do not work for them, do not promote them and avoid them getting near holding executive level political office where we can. These people know the difference between right and wrong, but choose to place self-interest and personal aggrandizement ahead of all other factors; they can only demonstrate loyalty to those who admire them. Anyone who disputes their glory is despised.

Hello Nigerians, it is time to beware of the gap between intent and impact. Leaders cannot just understand only the Nigeria dubious politics. There is a need for an understanding of how banking, finance, real economy, trade, healthcare and well-being, overall sustainable development, human capital development and many others work. It is true that the best predictor of the future is the past. But what past performance should count? Many of the current class did deceive the country and communities in recent past. Clearly it is best if the performance is recent rather than decade ago. The president, governor, legislator can't fix what he or she can't comprehend. People operating with a comprehension deficient syndrome with a dab of narcissism and delusions of grandeur do not have great record of reinforcement in making good decisions.

What, not Who, are You Voting For?

Nigerians are angry, and to reject the anger of today as something that is unwanted and destructive for the experiencing individual self and the overall social fabric will be a serious mistake. Hence, it is important that we discover the ways of understanding and using anger as an apparatus to advance quest for good governance in the country. *Do you know of someone who knows the 'right' way and all other ways are 'wrong?' Are they cocky, lack empathy, and think they are largely important? Never ready to admit responsibility. Such person wouldn't accept existence of perspective taking (the ability to adopt the perspectives of other people and see things from their point of view while suspending your own feelings or opinions). Then, it's possible he or she may be living with dab of narcissism and delusional disorder.* Such politician doesn't serve the people; he or she serves themselves. Then, for the good of our country, our states and local communities, SUCH PERSON should not come to the position of ultimate power.

We must stop the nonsense claim that there are no alternatives at this time to the present bunch of guys. An uncritical approach to a leader is always unhealthy. Narcissism is awful and very common in political leaders, but it's not a disqualifying criteria for governing. However, when we think about our families, our regions, and the community of the entire Nigeria, it becomes obvious that the question of pathological behaviour matters and question of leadership matters. There are things that are objectively wrong, for example. Narcissistic collusion is becoming common in Nigeria. Followers are so devoted to certain leaders who have narcissistic personalities that the latter can direct the follower to self-destruct and they would oblige. In such relationship, there is a strong bond between the leader and the follower that is not susceptible to reality.

Every accomplishment starts with the decision to try. I think there has to be much more active public participation in pushing our politicians in the right direction. This book is written to do that.

13

Leaders Embracing Uncertainty Is Critical

Each at their own time, each at their own pace, each in their own way.
Coming out is a process, a journey, not a race. Unlike most journeys,
there is no one destination in mind, only a direction. Keep on. When
you stray, or slow down, don't be afraid to ask advice or direction.
Your journey is yours alone, and regardless of where you end up, or
when, don't let anyone else plan the trip.

Steve Basile

If words of command are not clear and distinct, if orders
are not thoroughly understood, the general is to blame.
But if his orders ARE clear, and the soldiers nevertheless
disobey, then it is the fault of their officers.

Sun Tzu [Wu]

GIVEN THE UNCERTAIN TIMES WE LIVE IN, nothing can be taken
for granted. Much of the country seems to be in a state of bewildering
confusion. Nigeria today is both less secure and more vulnerable than in
most of her short history. Opportunities to get things right are
enormous. They roll in, at high-speed, in sets and intervals that mirror
the ocean's cycles. Opportunities available in Nigeria and for Nigerians
are increasing. We need the three arms of government working together
to meet the challenges in the dangerous and complex environment we
are living in.

Going forward, how Nigeria handles opportunities available to
her comes down to preparation, persistence, and purposeful passion, all
of which are traits needed by leaders and the people. It is time we elect
ONLY people who understand that winning election doesn't mean the
end of the game; it means the game is becoming more complex and
demanding. This means that in order to perform at the 21st century
level, the three arms of government needs to keep upping its game,

reforming its institutions, improving its strategies, and preparing itself to address more complex and challenging issues - at a faster pace than before, and with higher penalties for getting things wrong.

I wasn't here at the time, but I read former Prime Minister Abubakar Tafawa Balewa clearly when he said *"...Nigeria has now reached a critical stage in her history. We must seize the opportunity which has been offered to us to show that we are able to manage our own affairs properly. Every Nigerian, whatever his status, and whatever his religion, has his or her share to contribute to this crucial task. I appeal to all my countrymen and women to cooperate with me and my colleagues to create a better understanding among our peoples, to establish mutual respect, and trust, among all our tribal groups, and to unite in working together for the common cause, the cause for which no sacrifice will be too great..."* This was said over fifty years ago but is still relevant to this day! I am inclined to say to the present political leaders that winners takes all will not get us to that intended nation. Self-glorification is not what is needed. As someone said, "if you want to preserve yourself, you must preserve your opponent." Country is what really counts. But it is not in our reasoning and attitudes.

It's easy to be a leader when everything is going great. The challenge is how you act when things go wrong. In times of great change... or tremendous challenge... that's when the leadership fundamentals matter most. Our culture tells leaders that they have got to know and it tells them in so many ways, that uncertainty is bad. This chapter takes a decidedly different tactic than the prevailing culture. The core premise is that in many situations, it is in fact better to embrace uncertainty rather than eliminate it. This book encourages our leaders at all levels of government to aspire to embrace uncertainty. Why not? Accurate predictions are delusion and it is strength to admit not knowing. The chaos, complexity, and speed of change in the country require that effective leaders become masters of embracing uncertainty. When the seas are rough, you need the anchor of strong values, and the beacon of imaginative vision, to stay afloat. Appreciating late Winston Churchill's observation that when great forces are on the move in the world we learn we are spirits not animals. And there is something going on in time and space and beyond time and space which whether we like it or not spells duty, is the deepest obligation of every citizen at this material time.

Leadership in turbulent times... Candidate Labeling

Hello Nigerians, it is essential that we stop the practice of candidate labelling. Candidate labelling ignores the fact that views and values are shifting in response to ever-changing circumstances in a fast-paced world in which policy responses to emerging challenges require compromise. Constantly saying that all other people especially opponents are corrupt when no court of law have said so, are crimes against humanity.

Improving the quality and credibility of political leaders is essential to enhancing electoral democracy's legitimacy. We need more credible elective position candidates from presidential down to local government jurisdictions. When and only when we start to evaluate candidates on the positions of their possible leadership deliverable, capable people will not show up. It is important that we watch for what's coming, or we may miss future opportunities. In a world with a lot of chaos and uncertainty, a person worthy of leadership responsibility must have the ability to identify talent and understand complexity to be a success. While no one knows for sure what the future holds, we can make calculated bets on what will be. New generation of Nigerians has the potential to be the most powerful in history.

As I sat in a rather uncomfortable chair watching President Muhammadu Buahri deliver his administration 2018 Federal Budget statements to the National Assembly; I noted that he was notably more forthright and aggressive. However, I think the timing was significant. President Buhari in my honest opinion is doing all he can to fulfil that noble role "of helping people face reality and mobilising them to make change." And frequently people act with a certainty that only crumbles when the brute force of reality extracts its inevitable vengeance.

At the end of that particular President Buhari speech, an ever important sentence by *Dwight Eisenhower that "optimism and pessimism are infectious and they spread more rapidly from the head down than in any direction,"* was evidently manifested. The President's statements on the day and the performance of the budget approval processes reaffirmed the notion that anybody who is in a leadership role is [shaped] by his or her history and culture and in turn [also] creates the culture. It's not an either/or process. Saying it in another way, someone who evolves out of a certain milieu carries the nuances of that milieu or that culture and, in turn, will transcreate, and impacts the culture. It is obvious that the transformation has not happened. Transformation is hard. Real change requires evolution not substitution. It requires constructive disruption and not passivity.

Going Forward

This book has to be written. And I am lucky to have done so. I was/am very interested in what President Buhari has been saying lately because much of my work in the private sector and the public sector has been around delivering results based on what you make a commitment to do.

Just as it is critical for leaders to take a forward-looking perspective, citizens with an opportunity to choose leaders must take a forward-looking perspective. Good people, future focused voters try to forecast events and then influence them by their actions and decisions. Yesterday needs is what it is – past. Today's and tomorrow's needs must be adjudged differently, particularly in a fast-changing world.

The actions of today's leaders create the reality of the future – and its success or failure. Nothing stands still – change is a constant feature of life. Our choice of leaders today determines our welfare of tomorrow. So when you go to the voting booth or make other choices in life, you may want to think more selfishly. Think about yourself. Which candidate, policies, and choices will actually improve your life and which will hurt you? *Yes, Nigeria is in a crisis situation. I ask you now, are the people you are voting for and supporting to win and lead capable of changing themselves?*

Continual learning is also one of our greatest tools for progress. I ask you, are those you are considering for leadership position have the capacity to relearn. Actively engaging with the challenges that we face rather than being avoidant allows us to course correct and discover productive ways ahead. I ask you, is your choice of president, governor or legislator associate more with passivity?

14

Nigerians Wants More than One Vice President and with Executive Responsibilities and Accountabilities

Do not go where the path may lead, go instead where
there is no path and leave a trail.
Ralph Waldo Emerson

Tout le Sang qui coule est rouge! (All Blood Runs Red)
Eugene Bullard

BAD GOVERNMENTS BEHAVE BADLY, no matter what. What is also bad in Nigeria case is that as a people, we do not manage our leaders well. Be they president, governor, legislators, they endlessly misbehave. Everywhere you look, you see mini- disasters and failures. There is a Greek proverb saying that: "A society grows great when old men plant trees whose shade they know they never sit in."

The current federal government efficiency and democratic decision making are to some extent contradictory. Most Nigerians are advocating for a system where the country base its development on its own history, culture and on-the-ground reality. You are probably right with an opinion that the political system in Nigeria is a fraud and our presidency is dysfunctional and our various gubernatorial 'small lords like' are equally dysfunctional. How else would one describe a system that oppress and torment majority of the citizens. Where is our conscience? We must be worried for the future of the country; as the future is always made of the same stuff as the present.

"The law, must be honest, just, reasonable, and according
to the ways of the people. It must meet their needs, and apeak
plainly so that all men may know and understand what the
law is. It is not to be made in any man's favor, but for the needs
of all them who live in the land. No man shall judge [condemn]
the law which the King has given and the country chosen; neither
shall he [the King] take it back without the will of the people."
From the Danish Code of Jutland in 1241

Good people with presumed personal integrity are great to have, but good people do not mean effective government and good governance. The silent antidemocratic movements in and around the government are driven by collective narcissism. It is definitely time to say a big NO to all the useful people of low intelligence in the government and at the corridors of power.

As I began work on this chapter, President Muhammadu Buhari has confirmed his candidacy for oncoming 2019 general election. If you have followed the activities of his administration in the past three years as I have, may be the saying that leadership style is innate to a person would ring true in your ears. If that is true, one can rightly say that the country behavioural and situational factors are influencing many of the president's numerous successes and failures. Leaders can't always change their style to fit changing situations but they should.

I must remind Mr. President and all those appointed to position of power, that, in practice, strategy occurs interdependently - the result of cooperation and interrelationships in an environment such as ours that are neither inert nor stable, let alone predictable. The saying that secret of freedom is courage is ever true.

Make Nigeria Grow Again After This

Many don't want to accept the truth because it means hard choices have to be made, but the reality is that the current leadership structure is at war with our desired liberal democracy. If we don't respond with a new long-term strategy, collective narcissism, public office corruption and lack of intra-regional deficiencies can only be deteriorating more.

Nigerians have argued against the large responsibilities assigned to the presidents and the continuous growth of the duties. The vastness of the duties made it almost impossible for one person to fulfill the expectations placed upon it. *DO you think Nigeria should redesign the Presidency to better manage the uncertain and dynamic new world we have now, is a common question. And Nigerians are saying YES. Is collective presidency the answer? Nigerians are saying YES.* The country has become so complex that no one person can juggle so many balls in the air at the same time. The idea is that collective presidency will serve the country better. The responses received reminded me of a wonderful slogan of a certain Bill Clinton and Al Gore presidential campaign:

> We can no longer afford to pay more for – and get less from – our government. The answer for every problem cannot always be another program or more money. It is time to radically change the way the government operates – to shift from top-down bureaucracy to entrepreneurial government that empowers citizens and communities to change our country from the bottom up. We must reward the people and ideas that work and get rid of those that don't.
>
> Bill Clinton & Al Gore: Putting People First Campaign

Nigerians agreed that the offices of our president are very powerful and changes should be made. Extraordinary power not only corrupts, it encourages distraction, nepotism, hubris, narcissism and excess as well as growing resentment by citizens when that vast power fails to deliver. The country has become so complex that no one person can juggle so many balls in the air at the same time. Two heads are better than one, period. Nigeria needs more than one vice presidents with constitutionally guaranteed executive level responsibilities forming what other authors have called collective leadership system or collective presidency. This is a system that embodies institutional memory, consensus-oriented decision making, and shared responsibility. And given increasing age of our leaders, the thinking is that a collective presidency could better manage the scheduling rigors of domestic political consultations and international diplomatic forays than any single leader. If what it will take to fully understand the depth and breadth of Nigeria's poverty crisis, and how to uproot it "is a collective presidency," I am for it.

Change the Team – Be Ready to Say You are Fired!

Leaders are always captive of the people besides them. Among the powers of the president none is more useful than the power to appoint and fire federal officials. The shaping of presidents or governor's actions and image is greatly shaped by the actions of those in his inner circle, i.e., ministers and top-level advisers who represent the president's views. Please no president of Nigeria should ever tell us that he or she doesn't know this and that about his or her ministers and advisers and goes on to take action to know.

Every exit is also an entrance. The end of one thing is the beginning of another. Stay with President Buhari or your state governor or legislator or move on in the next election cycle. Either way, there will be new unintended consequences. In many ways, voters are the eternal optimists who can't learn from experience. But it is time for Nigerians to start learning and learning fast if we are ever to move up the ladder in governance effectiveness. Effective governance in smart countries is a baton pass, not a decapitation.

President Buhari like him or hate him [not that it matters to him or supporters], I want to think, is definitely making sustained progress or knowing what progress looks like. All of this leads me to believe: the wind is back in Nigeria's sails. We now have a window of opportunity, but it will not stay open forever. Let us make the most of the momentum, catch the wind in our sails. For this to be truthful, we should better chart the direction for the future. *As Mark Twain wrote – years from now we will be more disappointed by the things we did not do than by those we did.* Now is the time to build a more united, a stronger, a more democratic Nigeria for 2023 and so on. So throw off the bowlines. Let's therefore sail away from the safe harbor and catch the trade winds in our sails. We must be ready and prepared to disengage employed individuals who are not performing at the expected and desired level.

Get Ready for more Unintended Consequences

What do we want our federal and state *legislatures* of the 21st century to be? ... It's a question for the most part that has gone *unanswered,* and even *unattended.* One of the great things about getting older is you see things over and over again and you start to understand. That's called wisdom I guess. One thing I have seen over and over is that the best of intentions often lead to *unintended consequences*. Beyond the intuition that says "I know one when I see one," how do you go about measuring the effectiveness of any given legislature or presidency? What leading actions has President Buhari championed in his three years of presidency? Critics can find plenty of governing and ballot measures that have had unintended consequences. It is possible that President Buhari sometimes seems impervious to the second and third order consequences of his decisions.

We are living in the age of unintended consequences. Every person I know have had to struggle with the chasm between promise and possibility. Every president, governor, or local government chairman in Nigeria all through our histories have struggled with the gap between promise and possibility. We elect legislators to help legislate and make decent laws, but we ended up with people incapable of making decisions. We elect, so we thought, the president, the state governors to grow and secure our communities, facilitate economic growth and transformation, but we most times end up with people incapable of making truthful decisions.

It is lack of long-term expertise that forces political leaders to rely on special interests, or defer to bureaucrats, instead of making independent decisions. As other presidents we have had, President Buhari have millions of Nigerians supporting his policies. But in the deeply interconnected arena, the devil is always in the details and the implementation of some policies may do more to hurt than help the people who put their faith in him to fix their problems.

We want to believe that our politicians will improve our life; but post-election reality hits, the outcome are different. You do all you can to help sell their candidatures, elect them and you are paid back with so much "Us" vs. "them", cultivating fear and hatred towards out-groups that are deemed different (ethnically, ideologically, religiously, etc.), and vicious and virulent attacks against them. These are all part of an unsettling picture of growing ethnic and religious hostility in our dear country today. WHEN shall NIGERIA become a nation?

Looking Forward

History and science are the greatest learning tools. Complaining which we are very good in Nigeria is actually a violent move to inaction. All it does is replacing the need to act. This book is written to address the constant complain in the public domain. If we vote correctly and the votes are respected, it will definitely lead to good leadership and effective government.

A story was told that doing everything right ended up for presidential candidate Senator Hillary Clinton as doing everything wrong – and ensured one of the greatest upset in American political history in 2016 general election. President Buhari for all intents and purposes very much has the time to make his own history. He must make sure the intended consequences of outcomes of his actions are not unintended consequences. May I also add that it is not a weakness or disloyalty to dismiss an appointed officer who is not performing to the expectation of the employer? Mr. President, if my information is correct, it is only the Vice President among all the federal government employees that you need permission of the people to sack! Nigerians are watching some of your appointed officials and they are seeing issues of poor performance and insubordination, refusal to follow your directive issues. Historical norms, not laws, govern much of what we think of as appropriate conduct. Politicians want to be partisan – it's what gets them elected – jurists and law enforcement agents shouldn't be.

The number one reason people are fired (is the same as the reason they were hired). And that reason is personality. This is why Presidential and Governorship politics matter. This is why Legislative politics matter. We're not just choosing a President every 4 years; we're choosing a legacy, and a future. Hello Nigerians, when you get into that voting booth, remember that our actions of today determine the outcome of tomorrow.

15

Great Leaders Don't Need Experience

Simply, you cannot possibly know what I know unless you've made
the same mistakes or listened to my stories. Nor can I know what you
know unless I've solicited them from you. Sharing – it's how we
make our modifications and adaptations.
Lou Hayes, Jr

You can be disinterested in Politics, like me, but you can't
afford to be disinterested in Governance.
Joe Abah

THE CURRENT PRESIDENT WILL ONE day be out of office. The
current Senate President will one day be out of office. Nigerians are
starting the turn toward another presidential, gubernatorial, and
legislative elections. Candidates are announcing their bids and pundits
are practicing their rhetoric. But despite my faith in the qualified
electorate, so many Nigerians are worried. It's not any specific candidate
or issue or political ideology that's the source of the concerns. It's the
way we value certain leadership qualities - like perceived experience and
integrity – over traits like motivation, motional courage, competence,
character, and coachable potential when we go to the voting booth or
voice our supports. Sometimes an elective office candidate's potential is
obvious, but more often, as a voter, you have to dig a little to learn
whether someone is ready for a public office leadership role, and if
presented with multiple candidates, you have to evaluate which one is
best for the needs at hand. It isn't easy.

In the next general election, there will be no lack of challenge on
the choices available. Nigerians are saying that lack of both political and
military service experience should not be a show stopper. Quality
matters. Nigerians are looking for quality individuals. But what most
people mean when they discuss the quality of an elected or appointed

leader is a person's ability in a wide variety of areas. Intellectual skills and substantive expertise are essential. Political skills—prowess in dealing with the press, national assembly, the courts, state and local officials, and interest groups—are also key. Requisite managerial skills are many and varied: planning, organizing, and motivating employees in a bureaucracy, creating open communication with subordinates and good working conditions for employees, and developing administrative strategies for accomplishing the president or governor's goals. Strong interpersonal skills include personal stability, a sense of self-esteem, flexibility, a tolerance for conflict, the ability to accept criticism, and a sense of duty.

To help you make the decision, this book is written. A sign someone isn't supposed to lead is when they do not own bad results as well as good ones. This book encourages you to ask yourself questions on each candidate in the ballot. For instance, who among the gubernatorial candidates do you consider inspiring and why? All the book asks of you is to weigh carefully all of the ideas that are being advanced for your consideration and your well-being. Weigh them and if at any time they offer something that seems to spell out some kind of freedom from disaster, some freedom or security, but in return you must give up some of your right to choose as an individual then you make your mind up that the price is too high. Never give up your right to vote for a candidate of your choice.

There is reputational advantage in pragmatism. It pays to be hard on principles but flexible in the details. We must keep exploring. We must keep dreaming. Keep asking why. We must not settle for only the candidates we already know. Perhaps this is just an education problem. Maybe we will learn our lesson from the present presidential administration, national legislative houses and almost all the state administrations, and promise ourselves that next time we will select better. Maybe next time, we'll ignore the siren sound of big, sweeping promises that sound too good to be true because they are too good to be true. Maybe next time, the media will focus more on policies, less on personality, so we don't all get swept up in the drama. Everyone wants integrity, of course. We are so misinformed and ill-informed. Let's do something about it.

Why Not the Best? Great Leaders Don't Need Experience

Muhammadu Buhari was sworn in as president on May 29, 2015. At time, the immediate priority for Buhari was to instill, in fact, restore confidence in national governance. It was clear that the accumulated misgivings over the years tilted the balance inordinately as seen in the ballot box, and Nigerians were very happy to have acclaimed man of integrity with so many years of mini-political, appointed and career leadership experience. The slogan around the country was vote for people with experience. Fast forward to 2018, Nigerians are saying YES to "Not Too Young To Run," must mean not too inexperienced to lead. Our current leaders are public office experienced incompetent persons insensitive to average suffering Nigerians. Our nation is heartbroken and angry and yet we remain silent. Why? Shame on all of us! Today, we are reaping the benefits of electoral decisions. We don't have any action. We need to take action.

So be it. There's no law that a sitting president, a governor, a senator or a presidential candidate has to document his or her intelligence. But there is also no law preventing the people from asking and judging how smart and intelligent a president or governor or legislator or local government chairman or councilor candidate is for us to elect him or her as a leader. It is time that we start electing based also on potential and not just the faked perceived experience.

So many authors have written great books on the subject of experience and leadership. Do Presidents Need Experience? Gautam Mukunda wrote a book that tries to answer two vexing questions: *Does it matter which leaders we choose? And if so, can we make rational choices? "In Indispensable: When Leaders Really Matter,"* the Harvard Business School professor argues that 'unfiltered leaders'- those who haven't had much relevant experience - will likely have a greater impact than filtered leaders. What's harder to predict is whether that impact will be good or bad.

The idea here is that leaders (political, business, and military leaders) are vetted, or as Gautam Mukunda suggests, 'filtered' – he defines this as an insider who climbs up the ranks in a normal progression. His term for outsiders is 'unfiltered' leaders who, "either were outsiders with little experience or got their jobs through fluke circumstances". He then compared the groups' effectiveness; for instance, with U.S. presidents, he looked at historians' ranking from the past 60 years. He discovered that the unfiltered leaders were the most effective – and also the least effective – while highly filtered leaders landed in the middle of the pack. Filtered leaders will usually make basically the same decisions. Even if they are good decisions, their leadership doesn't have impact.

Unfiltered leaders according to Mautam are high risk, high reward. The things that made them so effective, such as their ability to think differently and not feel beholden to a certain way of doing things, often lead to terrible results. If you want to grow to dominance, you need an unfiltered leader, someone who will think differently and take risks.

Mukunda's research suggests that highly filtered leaders tended to perform the most consistently in the middle of the pack. That is to say, they are neither great nor horrendous. In essence, experience would be a good predictor of mediocre performance. NIGERIA is actually in a mess in almost every index of economic and social development. Filtered leaders in our midst have not got the critical thinking capacity required to bring us out. Research suggests that the best leaders tend to be outsiders who don't have a great deal of experience. Filtered leader would perform best in stable environments while unfiltered would better adapt to the extreme or sudden change. Nigeria is living in chaos Nigerians are asking in every level of our government for unfiltered activist leaders, who would feel free to disrupt the status quo.

Leadership it is said doesn't matter much, until the rare moment comes when it's the most important thing. A popular twice-elected governor of Anambra State, Governor Obiano is an ultimate example of the unfiltered leader.

Looking Forward

It is said that the presidency to an extent, is often a job for which everyone arrives unprepared. But just how unprepared is unprepared enough? What if the problem isn't the president—it's the presidency. The same is applicable at the state level. You learn that a leader without followers is simply a man taking a walk. In a way, Nigeria doesn't have a crisis of leadership; it has a crisis of followership. We want change, but we keep putting people or allowing people to put their own people in to bring about the change. Then the change doesn't come ... because we're putting people in that don't understand compromise or economic transformation and growth.

President Buhari in the past three years has done excellent in so many areas. The task now is to make sure that the future look like the best parts of the areas he has done well. And we can.

Where are the transformation-oriented Nigerians? I know we have you in every part of the world. Decide to organise and come together to move the country forward. I'm always interested in Nigeria's future and progress and its current situation. Are you? I don't see a better alternative. The political and governance system is really bad. We must fight to change the system. You and me must get interested in Nigeria party politics, though it can be as pig as in most places. They will put you off with their dirty ways. We must learn to wrestle with the pig-like system. Yes, we may get dirty, and the pig likes it when we do. But if we can educate our men and women on what qualifies transformation leadership, the pig-like systems are half way changed.

In addition, although the politics are sometimes played by men and women of dubious characters, they are not omnipresent. The more credible people like you (hopefully) stay away from party politics, the more poor governance flourishes. Let's therefore make the decision to interfere and be interested in politics. Having held an elected or appointed position before contesting and winning certainly does not guarantee a president or governor or legislator will perform well in the office. Let's therefore say NO to them who ONLY express boundless confidence in their ability to deliver on dubious airy promises and still seem to have a complete disinterest in the kind of policy details necessary to fulfil the promises. Nigeria as a country has to change direction in process and structure.

I hope you are with me on this: the only way a man can remain consistent amid changing circumstances is to change with them while preserving the same dominating purpose. For example, if we choose against ourselves in the next election cycle, we will have to live with the consequences and will have no one to blame, but ourselves. We must critically make better our thinking if WE ARE REALLY THINKING OF MOVING FORWARD.

16

Is Something Neurologically Wrong
With The Leaders?

There's enough for everyone's need, but not enough
for everyone's greed.
Mahatma Gandhi

You can't hate the roots of a tree, and not hate the tree.
Malcolm X

NIGERIA FEDERALISM IS PROVING TO be a recipe for disaccord and chaos, not accommodation. Too bad, though. It is very important that people see the presidency or governorship as a job, and a hard one, and it matters who got it. And if anyone is suited for any of the jobs, it's the hardest-working, truthful and healthy man or woman. It matters who got it. It matters how they do it. Think you can do a better job than the people who represent you? Don't just sit there – help fix the problem by running for office. But winning isn't everything. Character matters, too. This starts with leadership that appeals to Nigerians' best instincts and inspires them to be better. Yes, the quality of representation and the functioning of democratic institutions have become the central concerns to every well-meaning Nigerian.

Our people are still far-off in understanding what is required in picking the right team or changing existing team for good governance. Ask a question: can citizens achieve a basic knowledge of public affairs and then make reasonable choices about what to do? I can guarantee that you will receive multitude of opinions. I won't be surprised if your summarised answer is no. Those opinions will probably be over fifty percent plain lies. News and truth are not the same thing. It is essential that privileged educated among us devise a more democratic means to intelligently guide public opinion and facilitate conversation among and between citizens. This is what this book is written to contribute to.

Lies Are A Threat to Our Democracy + Good Governance

If we are to judge based on the quality of the effectiveness of the various administrations – past and present – we will not be far from the truth to opinions that unqualified candidates with disguised cognitive conditions may have been recruited. Why are Nigerians in certain positions of influence not acting based on principles and what their job definitions state? How can someone appointed or elected to public office lies about their job qualification certificates, what actions they are taking or not taking in their office? And when their various lies (or what Psychologist Bella DePaulo categorised as cruel lies — lies that hurt or disparage or embarrass or belittle other people; self-serving lies - help liars get what they want and avoid what they don't want, they help liars look better or feel better, or they spare liars from blame or embarrassment or anything else they don't want to experience; and kind lies - are the same self-serving, only they are told for someone else's benefit. When people lie to help you get what you want, or make you look or feel better, or protect you from something you don't want) are divulged, you and your sponsors mostly keep mute or repeat the same line of lies.

Reading and hearing some of the lies, it can be obvious that most does not appear to feel embarrassment or shame about lying. Accept it or not, cognitive control processes must be involved in deception among our public officer holders. The brain is dynamic and politics is said to alters our worldview and alters the way our brains process. Political Power is addictive and even more so in semi-authoritarian regimes such as we have in Nigeria where there are few institutional mechanisms to prevent abuses.

People can resign from their political appointed post based on principle. Not in Nigeria. In the past three years, so much filthy accusation of corrupt dealings under the administration of both President Jonathan and the current president by erstwhile and current public officials has become public. Ngozi Okonjo-Iweala's new book, Fighting Corruption Is Dangerous: The Story Behind the Headlines, draws on her years as Nigeria's Finance Minister provided pointers to different corruption cases and provided practical lessons on the difficult, sometimes-dangerous, always-necessary work of fighting graft and corruption. Only time will tell what will come out at the end of the current President Buhari administration.

I think that most Nigerians are living in denial on the state of the nation. Yes, it is true that resonant leaders attract, dissonant ones repel. As one of our political leaders, where do you belong?

As a confession to the shortness of life, I think we need to start doing much better NOW. We as citizens of Federal Republic of Nigeria have responsibilities here. The continual crisis of ethics and integrity in our government is surely a pathway to relinquishing our freedom. As President Obama once suggested: *"It falls on each of us to be guardians of our democracy; to embrace the joyous task we've been given to continually try to improve this great nation of ours. Because for all our outward differences, we all share the same proud title: Citizen."*

An academic colleague said a few months ago that (Nigeria is doomed to ineffective government and poor governance — that wrongheaded statement is an example of the destiny instinct, the belief that innate characteristics determine the destinies of countries or cultures) and it got me thinking deeper about our country. Will NIGERIA ever be a NATION? Nobody can predict the future with 100 percent certainty. I am a possibilist and the facts available convince me: it is possible.

I know that Nigerians are tired of politics as usual and are looking for leaders that can get out of their partisan corners to solve challenges facing our communities.

The complexity of the challenges facing us cuts across multiple domains - from internal security to high cost of basic food items to decay in our education to healthcare and well-being delivery. But many issues aren't in a silo. We need problem solving chief operating officers at the head of our government administrations. I think my academic colleague is wrong and I told him though at a later date - *the Nigerians instinct to see things as unchanging blinds us to the revolutionary transformations happening all around us.*

Let's Provide Neurological Examination

We have a political problem no one wants to talk about: *sick people in the ballot paper duly selected by their political party for election into position of influence and power.* There's no easy solution to the problem, but it demands a frank conversation. Tact and, perhaps, anxiety surrounding our own mortality too often short-circuit these conversations. Rumors regularly hit social media about the cognitive function of various politicians. The potential presence of mild impairments should not disqualify people from public office. These matters are hard to talk about in politics because they are hard to talk about in our own lives. However, it is very important that we start doing that.

I am an avid opponent to anything close to disability stigmatization. I am a firm supporter to the notion that we all have different abilities. However, I have seen enough in the past few years on the actions and inactions of some of the leaders at all the three branches of government that I now join Nigerians calling attention to the alarming absence of a system to evaluate elected public officials' fitness for office. One useful reform advocated by Nigerians is to subject all candidates for major office to a proper medical cognitive review from nonpartisan authorities. The results of this test will reassure concerned citizens that the 'leader to be' is not cognitively impaired and on a path of continuous decline. It is becoming essential that a testing format requiring comprehensive neurologic, psychological and psychiatric evaluation become constitutional decreed. It is very important that we know health status of would be state governor or president or legislator.

The lack of a system to evaluate candidate's fitness only stands to become more consequential as the average age of leaders increases and reduces. At a minimum, a simple test known as Montreal Cognitive Assessment (MoCA), created in 1996 by Ziad Nasreddine in Montreal, Canada can be utilized for that purpose. It's a relatively simple test that helps health professionals tell whether someone has an abnormal cognitive function - whether their ability to think is disturbed. Cognitive function refers to memory, speech, reading comprehension and the ability to learn new information. The one-page test takes about 10 to 12 minutes to complete. MoCA assesses orientation, short-term memory, executive function, language abilities, attention and visuospatial ability.

Today much more can be known about a person's neurological status, though little of it is as observable. This representation will obviously not be a very popular theory. *A nation is great not by its size alone. It is the will, the cohesion, the stamina, the discipline of its people, and the quality of their leaders which ensure its sustainable development and growth.* For that reason, I also want candidates of every age campaigning for any position to openly discuss their health issues. It's not dirty pool for reporters and political opponents to press them on such questions. We should address these matters without rancor or cruelty, but also without euphemism or undue reticence. While the field of candidates for the next presidential election is still taking shape, it is likely to include the youngest person ever to seek the office.

Looking Forward

I encourage you to keep a balanced but positive perspective on the democratic process for the sake of the next generation. For people at the pinnacle of power, there are too many judgments you have to make in this world that involve values, ethics and morality. It is known that high cognitive functioning is required to acquire and master larger amounts of knowledge, while moral integrity is needed to guarantee that habits and relations conform to the highest point of human dignity. The quality of candidates selected and elected impact ultimately on the quality of government delivered and the people can influence the quality of those leaders.

Apologies if you find this unbecoming. There are some people who like to sit back and admire a problem; I prefer doing something about it. Leaders respond to the actions of others, which meant a constant state of uncertainty, evaluation, and choice. *As Khalil Gibran once said, "March on. Do not tarry. To go forward is to move toward perfection. March on, and fear not the thorns, or the sharp stones on life's path."* For each of us, there are plenty of difficult obstacles in our path. Another of my favourite poems is *"The Road Not Taken." In it, poet Robert Frost introduces this thought: "Two roads diverged in a wood, and I – I took the one less traveled by, and that has made all the difference."* We have to make decisions every day of our life. And those decisions help direct us on our journeys. What paths are in front of you now? And which one will you choose to follow?

"We cannot navigate, without something to aim at and, while we are in this world, we must always navigate."

J. Gibson

17

Seek The Truth from Others And
Hold Them Accountable

Power is what men seek, and any group that gets it will abuse it.
It is the same story.
Lincoln Steffens

As I write this, I am certain that Nigeria will not be overcome by evil
people, rather, the good people of Nigeria will overcome
evil and Nigeria will be better for it.
Atiku Abubakar

WRITE A BIOGRAPHY OF AN AVERAGE NIGERIA public office
holder, and the emotional state expressed by most media anchors,
ordinary citizens, and absolute strangers to public service is: Why does
he lie so much? He must be corrupt. There are petitions against him or
her at EFCC. When bad things happened under his watch, he is never
held accountable and he never takes responsibility. To say that most
Nigeria politicians are incompetent, and in many cases downright
dishonest, isn't very controversial. We've all read about their blunders,
their tricks, certificate falsifications, and their schemes. So much false
accusations are out there and negative perception is said to be often
difficult to change. So many of our public officials past and present have
lived or living with so much potent and lethal attack against their
persons and go to bed every day with perceived battered reputation.

Yes, leadership in Nigeria is shrouded with deceit, dishonesty and
selfish acts. You hardly see leaders – not in Presidency, Governor's
forum, and Legislatures who sacrifice their authority, position and
incentives for the benefit of their people. None of them gives sincere
attention to how most Nigerians are struggling to feed families or find
work or builds a life that they could see from a distance but could not
quite reach. President Buhari built tremendous support in the rural

communities and suburban towns, in lands where farmers and artisans wanted to be heard. They viewed Buhari as a saviour and the most other politicians as a distant enemy. Is that very true. The "Whole Truth" must be a foreigner or foreign phrase in Nigeria.

Yet, to really progress and live in peace as one nation, Nigerians must learn to purge our minds and souls of acquired and accumulated bile. Politics and personal squabbles are often the cause of the various labels these public officials are tagged with. That has to stop!

So, then, what can we do? I'd say "think for yourself" since that's where change begins.

Going forward, it's important to seek the truth with relentless passion and with integrity... and hold our governing structures and governance to the highest standards of accountability.

The Truth demands our Attention

You must control your attention to control your life. Many leaders lure the people with hefty and airy promises only to be forgotten once they capture their leadership positions. And herein sits the ultimate explanation for leaders' habit: Most of them lie because they get away with it. What happens if, instead, we decide to stop lying and believing the lies from the so called politicians? The lies are not the problem. It's the millions among us who swallow them who really matter. Believers are the liars' enablers. Their votes give the demagogues their ill-gotten power. Let us instead choose to educate ourselves of the truth. The greatest hypocrisy is always to divert attention from what is staring you in the face today and may be kicking you in the teeth tomorrow.

Truth must be told to the leaders. It is our responsibility to see what is before our eyes, courageously, and to learn from it, even if it seems horrible-even if the horror of seeing it damages our consciousness. I believe I have the credibility to discuss these issues because I have been in the arena and I too have made every leadership mistake in the book during my journey. If I don't have no right to criticise a government or a leader, where do I derive the right to praise the government or the leader?

Former UK Prime Minister, Winston Churchill, must be right when he said that *"Criticism may not be agreeable, but it is necessary. It fulfills the same function as pain in the human body; it calls attention to the development of an unhealthy state of things. If it is heeded in time, danger may be averted; if it is suppressed, a fatal distemper may develop."*

I got really encouraged in this book project when I came across the following magnificent kind words from Teddy Roosevelt: *"It is not the critic who counts; not the man who points out how the strong man stumbles, or where the doer of deeds could have done them better. The credit belongs to the man who is actually in the arena, whose face is marred by dust and sweat and blood; who strives valiantly; who errs, who comes short again and again, because there is no effort without error and shortcoming; but who does actually strive to do the deeds; who knows great enthusiasms, the great devotions; who spends himself in a worthy cause; who at the best knows in the end the triumph of high achievement, and who at the worst, if he fails, at least fails while daring greatly, so that his place shall never be with those cold and timid souls who neither know victory nor defeat."*

What better aims and ambition can this book have for the good and long suffering people of Nigeria than the above inspiring words of Teddy Roosevelt?

This book is written to enable engagement and not avoidance. Nigerians are becoming more open to new ideas and majority are looking for leaders who walk the talk.

So I ask you you, is President Buhari walking the talk? Is Senate President, Bukola Saraki walking the talk? ARE Governor Patrick Okowa or Governor Ifeanyi Ugwuanyi and many others walking the talk? Are our former presidents and heads of states and state governors walking the talk?

Our inactions result in avoidance, not engagement with our supposed political leaders and statesmen. That avoidance might take the form of "effort minimizing" (i.e., people doing as little as needed to get by) or "putting up" with the leader. *A statesman according to Georges Pompidou is a politician who places himself at the service of the nation. A politician is a statesman who places the nation at his service.*

Give the President a chance to lead and hope for his Success
Give the Governor a chance to lead and hope for his Success

We must seek the truth. More to the point, the call to let the president, or the governor, or the Senate president lead and hope for his success fails to address obvious questions: *Where is he or she leading us to? How are we defining success? Should we applaud even if he or she "leads" us into another unnecessary conflagration? Are we expected to be happy if the "success" comes in legalizing nepotism?* However, it is partisan politics to plot a conspiracy of obstructionism to cripple his presidency or his governorship.

But at the end of the day, we know that politicians will always seek election. It is important that the people pay attention to what the people who claim to represent us are doing and saying in our name and on our behalf. The reason is simple. What worked yesterday will not necessarily work today.

Let's Take Our Country Back

It's time the majority that believes in a progressive, inclusive and compassionate Nigeria did more than just tweet or Facebook about it. The truth is beautiful and simple. Most of our leading politicians are becoming more neurologically closed to new ideas and it is bad for the future of our country. When engaged in a developmental discussion, a focus on what needs to be fixed, our privilege leading politicians becomes highly defensive; that is also not great for the future of our dear country.

I recently came across *Oprah Winfrey 2018 commencement speech for the USC Annenberg School for Communications and Journalism.* She had one question for the graduates and by extension for us as a people: *"What are you willing to stand for?"* This is question that is going to follow us for the rest of our life. In a stirring speech that called on graduates to seek truth and help others, the veteran television journalist, Academy Award-nominated actress, media multi-hyphenate and philanthropist offered practical advice, shared personal anecdotes and challenged students to tackle real-world problems. And I think it has some important life lessons on what we can do to help ourselves and our nation advance.

- Make the choice every day to exemplify honesty, because the truth exonerates and it convicts. It disinfects, and it galvanizes. The truth has always been and will always be our shield against corruption. The truth is our saving grace.
- Look for the lessons, because lessons are already there.

Hello political leaders and followers! Yes, we know that leaders needs and have constituencies. You must not, however, escape your responsibilities to the whole country or state. And let's not get too self-righteous. Leaders must come together, decide, organise to think and think better. All too often we become intoxicated by our words at the expense of our actions. But one thing is certain: The Nigeria leadership selection process is terrible. *THE HEALTH OF A SOCIETY is directly dependent on the quality of its leaders. This is simply true.* The inverse is also true. Where you find a society in disarray and suffering from lack of unity and direction, where majority of the people are not thriving and lack a sense of a common good, where they are incapable of hope and the lament of the mistaken direction of society is the common refrain, there you will also find a lack of good leadership. Either you are on the side of falsehood or on the side of truth, it is a personal choice!

Only language of tribal and religious politics transact in Nigeria. I was a victim of not belonging to the right tribe and religion and therefore your voting block doesn't matter. In a way, your personal contributions and potentials don't matter. I should have known better. I totally forgot the famous African proverb that "No one tests the depth of a river with both feet."

With that experience in mind, it became vivid to me what Edward Sapir had in mind when over a century ago, he said: *"Human beings...are very much at the mercy of the particular language which has become the medium of expression for their society. ...The fact of the matter is that the 'real world' is to a large extent unconsciously built up on the language habits of the group."*

Writing from Sao Paulo, the former Brazilian president Fernando Henrique Cardoso is definitely correct when he opinioned that representative democracy is in crisis. In his view at the core of this crisis *"is the widening gap between people's aspirations and the capacity of political institutions to respond to the demands of society. It is one of the ironies of our age that this deficit of trust in political institutions coexists with the rise in citizens capable of making the choices that shape their lives and influence the future of their societies."*

Going Forward

And Nigerians are looking for such leaders who are very outgoing and collaborative, creative, philosophical, visionary, and decisive in ever changing environments with blurred boundaries. Let every one of us exercise the constitutional power and vote only for nominees who understand what it is to value the impacts their actions have on the people. Let the path to peace be not diverged back onto the path to war. Issues of farmers and herdsmen have solutions and should be implemented. One death too many have happened and can be stopped. That is what we elected leaders to do and it is not a rocket science. A society that allows a situation like this to exist is plain and sick. There is power in spoken words. Don't ever confuse what is legal with what is moral because they are entirely different. Nepotism is wrong!

A famous statement of George Orwell is that "A people that elect corrupt politicians … are not victims … but accomplices.

"But I want to think that people who refuse to partake in electing credible leaders are the true accomplices. There is a possibility that we may be led by a largely cognitive unfit [and yet not receiving any proven therapy] group who are pathological and compulsive liars.

The country must run and run away from leaders and oncoming leaders who disguised as ideologues. Hope you know them. They are people who pretend they know how to make Nigeria, or their state or local communities a better place before they have taken care of their own chaos within. We must be wary no matter who is pedaling it or to what end. A simple-minded I know it all approach is no match for the complexity of existence; therefore, we are better without such people at the head.

You are nothing if you are not the truth. Beware of leaders who would teach you to fear. They would also teach you not to love, seek truth, or hope. They would rather weaken than strengthen, remain mute than communicate, and divide than unite. They serve their own ambition at the expense of the country. Nigerians wants votes only for people with evidenced critical thinking abilities.

Elections have consequences .... in the next general election cycle, inhumanity, ethnicity, nepotism, incompetence, corruption, lies, immorality and fraud must be on the ballot.

18

Leaders and Finishing Well

One is reputed generous, one rapacious; one cruel, one
compassionate; one faithless, another faithful; one
effeminate and cowardly, another bold and brave; one
affable, another haughty; one lascivious, another chaste;
one sincere, another cunning; one hard, another easy;
one grave, another frivolous; one religious, another
unbelieving, and the like. And I know that every one will
confess that it would be most praiseworthy in a prince to
exhibit all the above qualities that are considered good."
Machiavelli (Prince)

When one takes a position of leadership, there is a very
real danger of getting caught up in the hype surrounding
that status ... Surround yourselves with people who will
be honest with you about how you really are and what you
are becoming, and then make them promise to not
hold back... from telling you the truth.
United States Senator Ensign

TO SAY THAT WE ARE IN A MIDST OF NATIONAL brokenness is an understatement. The level of brokenness is not just in government but our society. The country feels fragile, chaotic, and full of conflicting realities. Ambiguity reigns, and radical uncertainty is lurking behind every decision. *Leadership creates culture.* After eight years of preaching change and hope, former President Barack Obama in his farewell address, ended his leadership with an urgent and fearful warning about the state of American democracy. *"If we don't create opportunity for all people, the disaffection and division that has stalled our progress will only sharpen in years to come," Mr Obama said.*

Hello Mr. President, Mr. Governor, Mr. Senator, it is helpful to start well as some of you have done, yet it is far more important to be able to finish well. To do both, one must begin with the end in mind. The clock is ticking for politicians aiming to shape the national future. *You can do great things, but in the process destroy people. And that is not leadership, very important to remember that. As President Obama said: "The absence of hope can rot a society from within,"* this book is challenging every Nigeria leader to have human capital development on top of his or her policy agenda.

As always, we are in an era of change, thus, leaders at all levels and tiers of government should better pay heed to the words of former United States President Abraham Lincoln, *who is reported to have called on his generation "to have the courage and foresight to change. The dogmas of the quiet past are inadequate to the stormy present, Lincoln said.* The occasion is piled high with difficulty, and we must rise with the occasion. As our case is new, so we must think anew, and act anew, Lincoln said." We have made progress in our democratic politics and must keep going. As President Bush asked in 2006, *"Today, having come far in our own historical journey, we must decide: Will we turn back, or finish well?"* The right answer is obvious. You can't leave it to chance. It's a deliberate approach that puts you back in control. Better education will result in good leadership and good followership.

Hello Mr President, Mr Governor, Mr Senator or Hon this and that, it doesn't matter if your intent is honorable if your impact is not.

As I have written elsewhere in this book, finishing well requires a high degree of imagination, creative analysis, and strategic thinking competence. These are what Nigerians wants each of you to have and be.

This chapter and the book will help leaders and citizens think anew about fellow Nigerians and how best to serve and what we need to have to serve well. Living on the numerous strong gut values discussed in the preceding Chapters of this book are essentials that will help you lead well and finish well.

Different people at different levels have argued on why and how we make our choices, but it is generally agreed that those are driven by emotions rather than by intellect. It is more important to finish well than to start well. If the Lord has called you to this position of power and influence – or to anything else - He has also called you to finish it. From where you are, let's all be able to devote time, attention and energies to be an activist for social justice, accountable governance and accountable leadership. It is a journey. We must not only speak for justice, but organise for justice, and act for justice. So, Mr. President, Mr. Governor, Mr. Senator, we must not only organise to bring down the forces of injustice but also organise to build, to put in place systems, processes, mechanisms that could work for the common good. It is in and on that spirit that this book is written.

In this Uncertain Times – there is No Time

With all the uncertainties, the greatest lie you can tell someone is that there is plenty of time. It is probably in Nigeria that at the age of 50 years old, you are still being told, no need to be too much in a hurry, it is just a matter of time, and your time will come.

I found the wise words of Martin Luther King, Jr. very comforting and indicative here. In a "Letter from a Birmingham Jail," King wrote about the need to understand the urgency of the present. A story was told that a white moderate - an ally of the civil rights movement - wrote to him saying that he, Dr. King, was in too great a hurry and that "the lessons of Christ take time to come to earth, are relevant here." African Americans, the moderate argued, would eventually be granted their full civil rights. Dr. King responded, and I quote: *Such an attitude stems from a tragic misconception of time and a strangely irrational notion that there is something in the flow of time that will inevitably cure all ills. Actually, time itself is neutral. It can be used destructively or constructively. More and more I feel that the people of ill will have used time much more effectively than the people of goodwill. We will have to repent in this generation not merely for the hateful words and actions of the bad people, but for the appalling silence of the good people.*

Unfortunately, the lessons of "Jesus Christ take time to come to earth," is the favoured attitude of most Nigerians political elected and appointed public officials. Why you may ask? Nigeria political leaders continue to be too comfortable with being comfortable. What is all the grandiosity from presidency down to local administrators all about? Nigerian opportune political leaders and officials needs to check their sense of self-importance. Their constant backbiting and public fight between the presidency and legislature is definitely not for the emancipation or betterment of the country or the greater well-being of the citizens. The constant public fight even under a government headed by President Muhammadu Buhari is really disheartening and is a testament that governance is never a priority for some of the political party and appointed officials. Hello political leaders, you don't have all the answers; this is understandable where meritocracy reigns; but nepotism is the norm.

The time to make the necessary changes in our attitude is now. There is no time left. Power is transient. You are here today, tomorrow maybe TOO LATE.

Hello Nigerians, do not dwell on the things that are happening right now. Don't worry about the things that have already happened. Instead, focus on how you can make adjustments, grow, and make the changes necessary to be ahead of the game. The former United States President John F. Kennedy was near perfect. He once said: *"Change is the law of life. And those who look only to the past or present are certain to miss the future."*

Hello would be Mr. President, Governor and Legislator, if you have humanity in you and you can hear and read; Nigerians are saying election cycle airy promises should stop. Nigerians are looking for real, concrete societal, economic and human capital transformation that would affect voter's everyday life and could easily be implemented and FOUR YEARS of service is long enough to make an impact. *And service is experiential.*

SO what do we do?

If we hallucinate that there is some saviour out there that's going to come along and make things better for us and clear up all the injustices, then that's just what we're doing: hallucinating - because it is not going to happen. Yes it's impossible to be sure about where we might end up in life but we have abundant tools to face the uncertainties. Nigerians are constantly deceived by the political leaders and political institutions. We must therefore learn to finish well in making that important decision on whom of all the elective office nominees to vote for.

In an increasingly volatile environment, leaders and kingmakers need to rethink talent recruitment to ensure that future elected public office and appointed officials are people with necessary capacity to meet changing needs. The Chinese, Americans, or Europeans are not coming here to do it for us. It's Nigerians that will make the required decisions to organize, and come together to solve our problems.

The current Vice President, *Prof. Oluyemi Osibanjo is very correct when he said: "Great economies and great nations, prosperity and abundance of nations and communities are created by men and not spirits. No matter how much you pray or fast our country cannot grow without some of us deciding to do the hard work that makes nations work."* To our amiable and professional Professor, I say to him and his team, "Well begun is half done," as Aristotle was quoted to have said. The most damaging phrase in Nigeria political language is: It's always been done that way. Too bad. All movement is not forward.

WE Must learn to Finish Well

Without getting too nostalgic, it seems to be a while since we have had some "real" people with a sense of community, intelligence and emotional courage to do the right thing for our communities and not just to win the next election, and the ability to convincingly explain why a decision was the right choice to make. Granted, this combination of gut values is a big asks and many politicians simply don't make the cut, yet it is the responsibility of political parties to ensure that potential leaders with these skills are recruited into the Presidency, Governorship, and Legislatures. The elected must also make sure that appointed officials has the necessary values to carry out the implementation of desired policies. When the parties flip-flop on that responsibility, when they indulge in internecine warfare and factional trade-offs aimed at getting one of their own into the top spot instead of capable leaders, then we end up with barely competent leaders that we are sometimes saddled with.

The truth is that everyone wants to be successful in life, but another truth is many people never really achieve what they set out to accomplish. Many of us fall short of obtaining our dreams and goals. This is true in life and leadership. Think about it. In almost any arena it is rare to see leaders who end their leadership lives with integrity and vibrancy. I am more convinced than ever that a leader will not finish well without great intentionality. Part of that intentionality should include understanding what could keep you from finishing well.

The concern for finishing well voiced by many Nigerians for our leaders launched me into a still ongoing study of the subject. What does it mean to finish well? Who did and how? Who did not and why? The preliminary results are highly instructive, personally challenging, and sobering.

Finishing well requires our conscience and integrity in discharging responsibilities in a manner that leaves no matters unresolved, e.g., unkempt promises. As a president or governor or Senate president, how much of your campaign promises are you keeping? You must value people fairly and equally in finishing well and is measured by the lives of people we have touched. Ultimately leaders must plan to work by the letter and spirit of the constitution of the country and norms of the position occupied. Our faithfulness to the rules and regulations of the constituting authority determines how well we finish.

I recently came across a very informative interview conducted by Forbes magazine with sportswoman, polar explorer and author of *On the Edge, Alison Levine,* on the subject of finishing well:

According to Alison, most of the deaths on Everest occur on the descent - after a climber reaches the top. The reason so many accidents happen on the descent is because people use everything they have all of their energy reserves - to get to the top, and then they have nothing left in them to get themselves back down the mountain. Every year there are mountaineers who collapse just below the summit; many of them die there. Getting to the top is optional. Getting down is mandatory. You have to know yourself well enough to judge when it is time to turn around and head back down. And you need to make that call when you still have enough energy left to descend. The hard part is that quite often that turn around point is before you reach the summit. The number one goal of any expedition: come back alive. Number two is come back with all of your fingers and toes. Tagging the top of a mountain should never be the goal.

The goal isn't getting to the top. The goal is getting back down - finishing well. Many Nigeria government leaders at all levels struggle with finishing well. Ironically, success plants the seeds for derailment. Success encourages complacency and arrogance both of which erode character and obstruct growth. Finishing well requires a lifelong commitment to self-awareness and growth. And that means feedback. Any leader that struggles with openness to feedback is flirting with disaster. And elected officials in Nigeria are good at that.

Going Forward

As we've just discussed, the quest for success allows no rest. The good news is that it's up to us. It is bad news too, for choice brings with it uncertainty and a burden of responsibility. For many of our challenges, our problems will lie within the hearts, minds, and behaviour of people, and so the solutions will lie there as well.

Finishing well requires that we have a purpose driven life in our leadership responsibility. As a political leader or follower, good governance and excellent service delivery ultimately should be the main purpose. Has Nigeria started well? Is Nigeria nation forming well? Will Nigeria finish well?

A central claim of this book is that there are things you can change, things you cannot change that must be accepted, and some things that are simply unacceptable, which you will need to get away from. These are tough decisions and it takes a lot of years and wisdom to know when it's time to quit. *Denis Waitley was very correct when he said: "Change the changeable, accept the unchangeable, and remove yourself from the unacceptable."* A central claim in this book is that finishing well does not always mean a happy ending. We can finish well even when we do not get what we want.

President Barack Obama was blunt when he said a few years ago in one of his numerous tours of Asia: *"So it's wonderful if you have natural resources. It's wonderful if you're a big country with a large population. But, ultimately, how successful a country is, will depend on whether its people have the skills and the education and the vision to be able to use those resources effectively."* It is a shame he didn't find it meaningful to visit countries in Africa as many times in his Presidencies and influence as many of the African leaders as we had expected. Did President Barack Obama finish well?

Every Nigerian wants an effective government and good governance for the country. We can only achieve that by electing capable people into leadership responsibility and be responsible ourselves. Knowing that failure comes in different forms, I ask: *Will President Muhammadu Buhari finishes well? How well did President Obasanjo finished? How well did President Goodluck Jonathan finished? How well did Senator David Mark finished? Will Senator Bukola Saraki finishes well? How is Rt. Hon. Yakubu Dogara doing and will he finishes well?*

And they will finish well. All are very interesting. I think you will find them interesting too. And if you follow the lessons they teach with their lives, you will go a long way finishing well. Maybe not like they did, for their examples are both exceptional and diverse. To finish well at the end, we have to begin to finish well now.

19

Portions of Nigerians are Asking for Enlightened Democratic Authoritarians

Elected autocrats maintain a veneer of democracy while eviscerating
its substance. Courts are gradually stacked, media bought off or
bullied into silence, opponents find themselves facing
tax or corruption allegations.
Steven Levitsky and Daniel Ziblatt

Perhaps the biggest inconvenient truth of the current times is this.
We've been idealizing democratic and all-inclusive leadership far
too much, when the need of the hour is- and always
has been – autocratic, top-down leadership.
Rajeev Peshawaria

DEMOCRACY DIES IN DARKNESS, said Bob Woodward. Are we at risk of the liberal democracy falling off a cliff in Nigeria before it actually fortifies its place in the country development? Nigerian politicians now treat their rivals as enemies, intimidate the free press and threaten to reject the results of elections. They try to weaken the independence of the institutional buffers of our democracy, including the courts, the intelligence services and ethics offices. They try to use state-controlled media and private-controlled state influenced media to spread congenial narratives, manipulate electoral rules, tilt voter registration and jigger the elections themselves.

Nigerians said: Things have gotten so far-off track in this country; we need a leader who is willing to break some norms if that's what it takes to set things right. Nigerians want to be led by people with defined purpose and values. Nigerians are asking for autocracy with democratic characteristics —in particular, accountability, competition, freedom of speech, protection of rights (right to life), anchorage of functioning institutions and partial limits on power.

That authoritarianism seemed to suit many of our people in 2018 as an alternative is a bit odd. This idea of an enlightened democratic and yet autocratic is conflicting with our assumed wider desire; for a political system that embraces the rule of law and responds to the will of the people. A system where public office leaders are ready to accept criticism and is expected to act more responsibly when carrying out their responsibilities. This Chapter is one of those in this book that was nearly not done. The attraction of autocratic thinking is quite disturbing. But as Martin Luther put it, *"If you want to change the world, pick up your pen and write,"* I know it has to be written.

Nigeria political leaders must now begin to understand that the greatest strength of Nigerian democracy is an engaged citizenry and doing the right in the right way all the time. Do they have the emotional courage and insights to act boldly on those problems?

Still, it is important to understand the reasons for the sudden appreciation of enlightened autocratic leaders. According to the submissions, Nigeria's current brand of presidential politics is spawning a dangerous mix of crony capitalism, rampant corruption and widening inequality.

What we have now is situation where Nigerians are actually serving some of our leaders who at their introductory campaign messages claim that they are coming to serve. We are having an outcome where people have the no absolute right to attack the official actions of those serving them; and are expected not to hold them to a higher standard. Our politicians are too selfish and self-indulgent to compromise to get anything done.

We are having situations where campaign for election to public service leadership is becoming a popularity contest. In the real world, the best companies are run by enlightened dictators with the right values and skills. In that enlighten environment, the chief executive officer listened very carefully to their employees, but they have to do what is best for the company, employees, and shareholders. They have to make tough decisions and take responsibility when things go wrong. They expect that once the decision is made; everyone will comply - whether the decision was good or bad.

Yes, Support For Strong Leaders is on The Rise in The Nigeria!

Madness in governance may be the main cause driving people to authoritarianism. Nigerians are saying that available democratic institutions are nepotism infested, corruption infested and chaotic, and advantaged Nigerian's selfish behaviour is constantly gumming up progress. Love for a bit of authoritarianism among Nigerians is caused by anxiety; people are frightened by changes taking place in the communities around them and, in an effort to maintain the status quo they look to someone—anyone—whom they believe will impose order on the chaos that threatens to upend the country they envisage. As Malaysian Prime Minister, Mahathir Mohamad put it in 1992; "authoritarian stability" has enabled prosperity, whereas democracy has brought "chaos and increased misery."

A lot of Nigerians are of the opinion that paying too much attention to electoral politics is misleading. Elections have not given us democracy. Vote-buying – candidates handing out cash and other inducements to voters – is a recurrent issue, leading to the widespread belief that elections are fixed. According to this group of Nigerians, the optimistic democratic premises have unraveled. Economic success and societal prosperity have not followed the acquired political system. Nigerians wants more attention turn to good governance. Nigerians are not contented. Contented people don't have time for authoritarians.

Leaders can be dictatorial yet inspire and motivate if they listen and communicate effectively and honestly. *Are Nigeria leaders honest and enlightened?* Yes, our presidents have been authoritarian and most of our state governors are authoritarians. But are they honest, competent and inspiring? Some would want the country to believe that they are honest in their thoughts and actions. *Who want a competition between meritocratic leadership and popularity leadership model?*

Truth, reason, evidence, decency must all be sacrificed to the greater good of keeping the strongman looking strong.

Nigerians gave examples of what they are looking at. For instance, Oman is an enlightened autocratic sultanate. Most of the Asian Tigers including Singapore and Malaysia owe their rapid modernization and economic revolution to enlightened autocratic leadership. These countries were once headed by people inspired by unmatched patriotism and love for both country and citizens. They see power given to them by their people with sole purposes of using it for positive socio-political and economic transformations of their countries. They succeeded tremendously.

Maybe we need enlightened autocratic leaders! Just a thought! I really don't know!

But I know that leadership is generally recognised as influence from someone at a higher level of an organisation (and a country is actually one big organization). That influence is used to enable the organisation to achieve its goals. The term 'autocratic' refers to how they go about exerting that influence. The country must guide against the current manipulated majority opinion spreading in the country. The constant and persisting media induced self-righteousness is excruciating.

Personally, I am an optimist. I always assume things will get better. I wake up every morning thinking I will have a good day, even if I have something to worry about, like writing this book. Today the weather will be better; the next book I read will tell me some of the things I am trying to understand about my research project. Let's look around from East to West for inspiration and find out: "What works best?" and "Can it be applied here in our Nigeria kind of federation, in our states and in our local government areas?"

Now, what's your reaction to that!

We must be careful of what we are getting into. There is a Bengali proverb that said: *"when the king dies, it does not mean the kingdom stops."* The kingdom goes on. But when, so long, the leader or the person in charge remains there, he thinks that *"without me; everything will be spoiled."* This is called illusion. As in Kellyanne Conway *"alternative facts,"* there are always side effects to consider. It is time we sit and talk about truth and transparency. To autocratic thinking Nigerians, you may want to remember that autocratic leadership only works until it doesn't work. And then everything goes wrong; entire country can collapse. Remember, the fantasy of today is the reality of tomorrow, and lately our tomorrows have been arriving faster than we had ever dreamed. It was Gail Sheehy that said, *"If we don't change, we don't grow. If we don't grow, we are not really living. Growth demands a temporary surrender of security."*

Voting is leading. Elected officials are public servants. We must stop treating elected officials as if they are the hottest celebrity and start demanding sound policy offerings from them. It is time we start making concrete and evidence based electoral decisions.

Gaslighting will not develop Nigeria. In the interim, the class of 2019 leadership out of selfishness and indolence must not destroy NIGERIA as we have it now. It is possible.

I'm hopeful that despite all the noise, all the lies, we're going to remember who we are, who we're called to be. Out of this political darkness, I see a great awakening ...
Barack Obama

Progress doesn't just happen effortlessly. We make progress because of things that people do.
Paul Romer

20

Knowing It All Ends

Let each citizen remember at the moment he is offering his vote
that he is not making a present or a compliment to please an
individual – or at least that he ought not so to do; but that he is
executing one of the most solemn trusts in human society
for which he is accountable to God and his country.
Samuel Adams

If you open the door, if you create the political will,
I'll drive through that opening.
Lyndon Johnson

Lead me, follow me, or get out of my way.
George S. Patton

IN THIS BOOK I HAVE TRIED TO TRANSCREATE and synthesize what I have learned over the past decade from my research on values and skills, Nigerians are looking for in tomorrow's politician seeking an elective office. The result is a descriptive claim and a prescriptive claim. It is a book, by a professional optimist, about how personal responsibility or personal accountability by all citizens can bring about beneficial changes in both vertical and horizontal accountability. It was Marcus Aurelius who said, "Your life is what your thoughts make it," and those are the ideas expressed in this book.

Agreed, there is so much deceit, so much distortion in the country. Debate is still on that we are known to even dupe ourselves in order to deceive others, creating valueless social advantage. We live at an opportune moment. We have seen that change is possible and change represents opportunity. Nigeria has the talents, resources, and spirit to excel. Whenever any politician or fellow tries to convince you of something, think about what might be motivating that person. Throughout the book I have highlighted that where ordinary people get involved then good things happen in the process. Therefore it's to the benefit of the country that informed individuals share the knowledge with uninformed ordinary Nigerians especially of the voting age. This is a counsel of conscience.

'Make your voice heard', 'Are you with me'

Nigeria has teetered on the brink of catastrophe before, and rebuilt itself by rethinking its institutions. It's time to do so again. Leadership and governance, both good and bad, are universal political and social institutions. And Nigerians are tired of mediocre leadership and poor governance. The one thing I do know, however, is that there is a lot to be learned these days about leadership (or the lack of) from Abuja and other capitals and headquarters we have in our dear country.

Unfortunately, they are showing us more about what not to do in terms of leadership, than providing role models of true leadership. Nevertheless, a lesson is a lesson, and our politicians and policy managers are sharing some great ones right now. But Nigerians are getting smarter. As proved in 2015 general election, voters increasingly see themselves as voting against the party or person they dislike, rather than for one they do like. Next one won't be far from it. For the Presidency to succeed, others must not have to lose. It is important that we understand that there is a difference between values and policies. A 'good man' does not really get us to a 'good policy.'

The unnecessary fight between different organs of the government and between agencies of federal government sometimes feels like locking oneself in a dark room. No one will emerge as a winner in that war. We must learn to treat everyone with sincerity, warmth, attentiveness, and forthrightness. Sometimes it seems that the executive and legislative arms of government are den of warring cliques. People have asked and rightly so if some of them have any principles to defend. Some have habitual habit of speaking without saying something.

Arise O compatriots and let's make them establish norms of civility and tolerance and a commitment to reason and facts. It is time we sit and talk about truth and transparency.

The relationship between executive arm of our government and the legislators is becoming our failure, and while it's easy to scoff at them, it's more important to inquire into how we got to this point. The actions are symptoms. We are witnessing cultures bereft of ideas, politics without inspiration or principle. And most forget that even though the days seems to last forever, the weeks, months and years fly by. And that is very, very true. Power is finite and evaporates much faster than you expect.

What does it mean to be Nigerian?

The Nigeria I know and wants to be in is full of courage and optimism and ingenuity. The Nigeria I know and wants to remain in is decent and generous. Nigerians must get frustrated with political gridlock and worry about naked ethnicity, religious, 'us vs. them' divisions and madness.

Majority of Nigerians are victims of hyperbolic misrepresentation and to them, I say listen to the lessons in the *Martin Luther King's "Letter from Birmingham Jail: A Lesson for All." In that letter, despite the realities of 1963 America, Martin Luther King never stopped believing that things could be better, that the privileged would stand up for justice and the powerless would stand together to demand their rights. Even from the cell in which he was unjustly jailed, he wrote that those who bravely fought for justice helped to carve "a tunnel of hope through the dark mountain of disappointment."*

As King said, "the time is always ripe to do right."

We are a great country and hopefully a great nation soon. Decide to be a great Nigerian! The time is right now. Time for capable people to go for it! Government goals or policies must have purposes and not in conflict. Going forward, it is vital not to separate policy formulation from implementation as has been the case for so many years. People beside our president matters! People beside the state governors matters! And it's not just the people the president appoints — it's also who he and the rest of the administration consult. Every now and then a few disparate things collide, and suddenly you see a pattern. People must be sensitive to such pattern.

It is just so difficult not to be personal even in public life…. You can see why we have some shameless enthronement of ethnic-driven mediocrity in our government and public institutions. Yet every responsible person must adopt positions based on facts. I remember two of my wonderful friends – JOE and MARYAM asking me why this book? My answers - I have a deep love for our country and a concern about its future and that is exactly why this book is written. *Everyday life is a school of the spirit that offers us chance after chance to practice dealing with heartbreak. Those chances come when we aspire and fail or hope and have our hopes dashed or love and suffer love's loss.*

I have heard it said that being courageous is doing what you are afraid to do anyhow. But this time it felt more like what Ray Bradbury said: *"Taking risks is jumping off the cliff and building your wings on the way down."* One minute you are on top of the world. And the next minute, it may seem that the world is on top of you.

But nothing much happens without a dream. For something really great to happen, it calls for a really great dream. I want to think that we have to keep going. Tomorrow will never be a re-run of today. It is always different – always challenging. I am determined to make a grand effort to touch tomorrow today through the informal tutoring of others.

While no system is perfect, MARYAM, WHERE is that courage you built up over the years? It is almost inconceivable … unpublicised loyalty to old acquaintances is a fair indicator of character. It was our own *Maya Angelou that once wrote that "one isn't necessarily born with courage, but one is born with potential. Without courage, we cannot practice any other virtue with consistency. We can be kind, true, merciful, generous, or honest."* It's never late to begin.

I'm quite aware that many of the points in this piece may seem overgeneralised, or extreme. Fiction writer John Barth, when criticised about the liberties he took with his characters, replied paradoxically in his defense: "I exaggerate for the sake of truth." Hopefully, any hyperbole in this piece will be taken by the reader in the same spirit. This is another of my contribution to the national transformation. Agreeing or not agreeing with me doesn't change the facts. I believe that reason is fundamental to all endeavours. Unfortunately, all of us have what are called cognitive biases – we have ways of thinking about evidence that leads us systematically to misunderstand the way the evidence points.

Leadership is an obligation. It is a community, decision and is hard and from what we have seen over the past three years, it's getting harder. And without followership, leadership is nothing. Good followers are continually learning and updating their skills and abilities. We have to stop pretending that it is easy or that some quick-fix idea is going to make things better. We can see(or learn) from President Buhari's last three years showing that you need to develop the resilience and determination to tackle the hard work of leadership. And having the capacity to vote for a candidate in an elective democracy is leadership.

Leaders must learn to get the important things done and that can only happen where they understand the importance of avoiding distractions and have feelings about stuff around them. Change is painful and the road will not be easy. It was George Patton that famously said: "Lead me, follow me, or get out of my way."

To quote Jim Rohn, *"The way to enjoy life best is to wrap up one goal and start right on the next one. Don't linger too long at the table of success; the only way to enjoy another meal is to get hungry."* When faced with this situation, good followers and good leaders with the best intentions in mind have real courage and the assertiveness to confront wrongdoing and set limits on others.

I hope that my writing has proved useful to you. I hope it revealed things you knew that you did not know you knew. I hope the crowd wisdom I discussed provides you with strength. I hope it brightened the spark within you. The lessons of his book are rooted in realism. It is choice not chance that determines our future direction. My hope is that the gut values presented in this book will help you to do so even more effectively in the future.

Good luck and best wishes to you on the paths ahead.

Suggested Reading

1. Adams Family Papers: An Electronic Archive. Massachusetts Historical Society. Available at http://masshist.org/digitaladams.

2. Andrews, J. (2012). Barack Obama and Leadership: 10 Reasons the 44th President Squandered Unprecedented Goodwill. Jim Kochenburger, 2012.

3. Aronson, E. (2010). *Social Psychology.* (7 ed.). Upper Saddle River, New Jersey: Pearson Education, Inc.

4. Baker, N. (2014). The future is about people. The Futurist,2014 Issues of The Futurist, 48 (4), July – August. Retrieved fromhttp://www.wfs.org/futurist/2014-issues-futurist/july-agust-2014-vol-48-no-4/future-about-people.

5. Balewa, T.A. *Mr. Prime Minister: A Selection of Speeches Made by Alhaji the Right Honourable Sir Abubakar Tafawa Balewa, K.B.E., M.P., Prime Minister of the Federal Republic of Nigeria* (Apapa: Nigerian National Press, Ltd., 1964).

6. Bourgon, J. (2012) quoted in Ben Ramalingam "Aid on the Edge of Chaos", Oxford University Press, 2012.

7. Blair, T.(2011) A Journey: My Political Life, Vintage; Reprint edition (September 20, 2011).

8. Bregman. P. (2018) Leading With Emotional Courage: How to Have Hard Conversations, Create Accountability, And Inspire Action On Your Most Important Work. John Wiley & Sons.

9. Bufalino, G. (2018) "We need great "followers", not just great leaders: a brief questionnaire for followership development", Development and Learning in Organizations: An International Journal, Vol. 32 Issue: 1, pp.1-3, https://doi.org/10.1108/DLO-04-2017-0040

10. Bush, GW (2004) Decision Points, Crown Publishing.

11. Dewan, T, Myatt, DP. (2009) *On the rhetorical strategies of leaders:*

speaking clearly, standing back, and stepping down. PSPE working papers, 06-2009. Department of Government, London School of Economics and Political Science, London, UK.

12. Dorsey, GL (2008) "The Presidency and Rhetorical Leadership" Texas A&M University Press, 26 Mar 2008.

13. Eurich, T (2018) *Insight: The Surprising Truth About How Others See Us, How We See Ourselves, and Why the Answers Matter More Than We Think,* Currency; Reprint edition (June 5, 2018).

14. Ewan, BR (2010) An Introduction to Theories of Personality, 7th ed. New York: Psychology Press, 2010.

15. Freud, S. (1921). Group psychology and the analysis of the ego (J. Strachey, Trans.).London: Hogarth Press and the Institute of Psycho-analysis.

16. Galton, F (1907) "Vox Populi (The Wisdom of Crowds)," Nature, 75 no. 7 (1907), 450-451, http://www.nature.com/nature/journal/v75/n1949/abs/075450a0.html.

17. Gardner, H (2011) Frames of Mind: The Theory of Multiple Intelligences. New York: Basic Books.

18. Gautam Mukunda, (2012) Indispensable: When Leaders Really Matter. Harvard Business Press, 2012.

19. Genovese, MA (2016) The Future of Leadership: Leveraging Influence in an Age of Hyper-Change. Routledge: New York. Heffernan, M (2011).

20. Goldsmith, A (2005). How Good Must Governance Be? Paper presented at the conference on 'The Quality of Government: What It is, How to Get It, Why It Matters', Quality of Government Institute, Goteborg University Sweden, 17-19 November.

21. Graham A., et al (2013) Lee Kuan Yew: The Grand Master's Insights on China, the United States, and the World. MIT Press. 2013.

22. Green MJ (2004) Your Past and the Press!: Controversial Presidential Appointments : a Study Focusing on the Impact of

Interest Groups and Media Activity on the Appointment Process. University Press of America, 2004.

23. Gutmann, A, Thompson, DF (2010) The Mindsets of Political Compromise https://president.upenn.edu/meet-president/mindsets-political-compromise.

24. Haidt, J (2012) The Righteous Mind: Why Good People Are Divided by Politics and Religion. Pantheon Books, 2012.

25. Hargrove, CE (1998) The President as Leader: Appealing to the Better Angels of our Nature (Lawrence: University Press of Kansas, 1998).

26. Henrich, J (2015) The Secret of Our Success: How Culture Is Driving Human Evolution, Domesticating Our Species, and Making Us Smarter, Princeton University Press, 2015.

27. Jost, JT (2006) The End of the End of Ideology. *American Psychologist*, Vol. 61, No. 7, pages 651–670; October 2006.

28. Kahneman, D (2011). Thinking, Fast and Slow. Farrar, Straus and Giroux, 2011.

29. Kellerman, B. (2014). Hard times: Leadership in America, Redwood City, CA: Stanford University Press.

30. Krupp, S, Schoemaker, P (2014). Winning the Long Game: How Strategic Leaders Shape the Future. Public Affairs, 2014.

31. March, J, Olsen, J (2006)"The Logic of Appropriateness,"in The Oxford Handbook of Public Policy, ed. Robert E. Goodin, Martin Rein, and Michael J. Moran (Oxford: Oxford University Press, 2006).

32. Mills, CW (1956). The power elite. New York: Oxford University Press.

33. Moran, D (2011) If You Will Lead: Enduring Wisdom for 21st-Century Leaders. Agate Publishing, 2011.

34. Montreal Cognitive Assessment (MoCA) - Cognitive Screening Instruments - 2013 A Practical Approach. 10.1007/978-1-4471-2452-8.

35. Newell. T (2017) **What Is A Voter's Responsibility?** https://www.huffingtonpost.com/terry-newell/what-is-a-voters-responsi_b_12204454.html.

36. Northouse, P. (2013). *Leadership: Theory and practice.* (6 ed.). Thousand Oaks, California: Sage Publishing.

37. Palmer, J. P. (2011) Healing the Heart of Democracy: The Courage to Create a Politics Worthy of the Human Spirit, John Wiley & Sons.

38. Perruci, G. (2011). Millennials and globalization: The cross-cultural challenge of intragenerational leadership. Journal of Leadership Studies, 5(3), 82-87.

39. Renshon, SA, (1998) The Psychological Assessment of Presidential Candidates (New York: Routledge, 1998).

40. Rezvani, S (2010) The Next Generation of Women Leaders: What You Need to Lead but Won't Learn in Business School. ABC-CLIO Incorporated, 2010.

41. Skowronek, S. (1993) The Politics Presidents Make. Cambridge, Mass: Harvard University Press, 1993).

42. Sowcik, M, Andenoro, AC (2015) **Mindy McNutt, Susan E. Murphy** (2015). Leadership 2050: Critical Challenges, Key Contexts, and Emerging Trends. Emerald Group Publishing, 2015.

43. Surowiecki, J. (2004) The Wisdom of Crowds: Why the Many Are Smarter than the Few and How Collective Wisdom Shapes Business, Economies, Societies, and Nations (New York: Doubleday, 2004).

44. Turner, BS, Nasir, KM (2014) The Future of Singapore: Population, Society and the Nature of the State. Routledge, 2014.

45. WayneSJ (2011) Personality and Politics: Obama For and Against Himself, SAGE, 15 Mar 2011.

46. https://psychologenie.com/why-people-lie-psychology.amp

47. https://annenberg.usc.edu/news/commencement/oprah-winfrey-

urges-usc-annenberg-graduates-seek-truth.

48. https://qz.com/876260/seven-presidents-are-better-than-one-why-the-oval-office-needs-a-round-table/

49. https://www.psychologytoday.com/gb/blog/living-single/201712/how-president-trumps-lies-are-different-other-peoples

50. https://www.inc.com/linkedin/vivek-wadhwa/democracy-great-thing-except-workplace-vivek-wadhwa.html

51. http://www.foxnews.com/politics/2018/05/12/bloomberg-slams-pols-for-epidemic-dishonesty-calls-it-greater-threat-than-terrorism.html

52. https://chiefexecutive.net/embracing-uncertainty-leading-adversity/

53. https://www.huffingtonpost.com/brenda-m-cotter/is-authenticity-overrated_b_10020706.html

54. https://www.rand.org/research/projects/truth-decay.html

55. https://www.eisenhower.archives.gov/all_about_ike/quotes.html

56. https://theconversation.com/africa/partners

57. http://dailypost.ng/2015/05/29/full-text-of-president-buharis-inauguration-speech/amp/

58. https://hbr.org/2011/11/why-inspiration-matters

Index

www.ingramcontent.com/pod-product-compliance
Lightning Source LLC
Chambersburg PA
CBHW031958040426
42448CB00006B/407